# JIM'S LAST SUMMER

TERESA RHODES McGEE

# *Jim's Last Summer*

## *Lessons on Living from a Dying Priest*

ORBIS BOOKS
Maryknoll, New York 10545

Founded in 1970, Orbis Books endeavors to publish works that enlighten the mind, nourish the spirit, and challenge the conscience. The publishing arm of the Maryknoll Fathers and Brothers, Orbis seeks to explore the global dimensions of the Christian faith and mission, to invite dialogue with diverse cultures and religious traditions, and to serve the cause of reconciliation and peace. The books published reflect the views of their authors and do not represent the official position of the Maryknoll Society. To learn more about Maryknoll and Orbis Books, please visit our website at www.maryknoll.org.

Copyright © 2002 by Teresa Rhodes McGee

Published by Orbis Books, Maryknoll, New York, U.S.A.

Queries regarding rights and permissions should be addressed to: Orbis Books, P.O. Box 308, Maryknoll, NY 10545-0308, U.S.A.

Manufactured in the United States of America

Cataloging-in-Publication Data is available from the Library of Congress

ISBN 1-57075-420-9

# Contents

# *Early Summer*

I KNEW THAT Father Jim Lenihan had returned from American Samoa to Maryknoll, New York, because he was ill, but I did not know much about the details of his disease. I met him one day on a stairway. We shook hands, and he said, "You've lost a lot of weight. Are you all right?" I told him that I had been diagnosed a few years earlier with rheumatoid arthritis. The disease and the medications had totally taken away my appetite. Jim said he knew that the disease was very painful, and that he was sorry that I was suffering. He then said with his characteristic directness, "You know I have cancer." As I mumbled my sympathy he added, "Well, it's terminal."

Even though it was the way Jim would deliver such news, I was startled by the matter-of-fact way that he told me his prognosis. He didn't have the time or patience to do it any other way. Jim told me that he was going for more x-rays to determine the effectiveness of his radiation treatment. "It's only for the pain," he said. He told me that he would like to talk with me when he returned from the hospital. We agreed on a time, and I walked away touched and deeply saddened. The last thing I wanted to think about was Father Jim Lenihan being terminally ill.

When he sat down in my office a few days later, I noticed how gingerly Jim moved. The way his tall, thin body sat in the chair quickly reminded me that nothing could cure the cancer that he carried in his spine. "It doesn't hurt like it did," he said as he shifted in the chair. "But the radiation treatments have worn me out. I know that I need to go to the nursing home soon." With his characteristic sun hat in hand, Jim looked to me like the merchant marine that he had been during World War II. His hands and arms still looked strong; his vision was clear. Jim's thin, weathered face and bright blue eyes were, however, showing the effects of his pain. Seventy-three years old and terminally ill with cancer, Jim knew that the storm of his illness was only going to grow in intensity. Using one of his frequent references to the sea, Jim said that at that moment all he could do was look at the horizon with wisdom, care, and humor as his still point. Then, like a sailor caught in rough waters, he could measure where he was going. Cancer, he told me, was promising to have some "whopper" waves.

Jim came to see me that day to talk about writing. He asked me to read the autobiography he had written and tell him what I thought about it. I was pleasantly surprised by the invitation because although I had known and worked with Jim for almost a decade, I did not expect him to trust me to read his life story. But trust me he did, and I read the autobiography with great interest. I learned about the origins of the family in Ireland, Jim's formative years, the merchant marines, the seminary, and forty-three years of missionary priesthood in Africa. Jim wrote clearly, and it was easy to follow the story. His clearest writing, however, described his ongoing process of recovery from alcoholism. Sober for seventeen years, Jim believed that there was no greater gift than to be part of the rebirth of someone profoundly afflicted by alcoholism. He had helped thousands of people in his life as a priest, but one of his greatest sources of joy was having helped to establish Alcoholics Anonymous in Tanzania. Though I knew some of this information and was certainly aware of the joy he found in helping others into recovery, reading this material in light of Jim's terminal cancer moved me deeply. There seemed to be lessons in the writing for my body and my soul, tips about living with illness and striving for health. He treasured the people he had met through AA and wanted to share with the world the joy he knew in his own recovery. Locked as I was in my own experience of pain at that moment, I found that I was eager to read and hear of such deep joy in the face of imminent death.

When we met again I told Jim that I thought he had a great deal to say. I wondered if he had done additional writing about the principles and teachings of AA. He told me that he had "quite a few" papers on the spirituality of the Twelve Steps, courses he had taught, retreats that he had given. Much of it was in outline form. I encouraged him to write more from those outlines because I believed that other people would react to it as I had — they would want to learn more. I told him that at that moment in my life, more than ever, I needed to hear what he had to say.

He was pleased with my feedback. Then the years of working a program based on rigorous honesty became evident as he looked at me and said, "I don't think that I will have the time to organize the outlines and the writing. And I am positive that before long, I won't have the energy either."

So we talked for a while about his diminishing energy and he gave me more detail about his prognosis. Jim's cancer had been diagnosed eight weeks earlier in American Samoa. He had just finished writing the outlines for a major retreat that he was planning to give to the religion teachers in the area. Jim claimed that all of his best ideas had gone into that outline and he was greatly looking forward to teaching during the retreat. Before the retreat began, Jim went to the doctor to get the results of a chest x-ray. The test was done to rule out anything more serious than tropical heat as a cause for Jim's fatigue, loss of appetite, and back pain. The x-ray showed a massive, metastasized tumor on the spine. The original site was undoubtedly the lungs, which by the time of diagnosis were full of tumors. Jim asked for the doctor's realistic opinion. The doctor told Jim that the prognosis was very poor but that options were available for radiation to ease the pain and chemotherapy to buy him a little time. The extra time should be thought of in terms of weeks, not years. Jim had watched his sister go through agonizing chemotherapy to gain those weeks only to die in great pain from a similar type of cancer. It was an experience that Jim did not want to repeat. "I want to be kept as comfortable as possible," he said, "because it looks like God's plans are a little different than mine. I've spent years trying to get Jim's plans to match up with God's plans and now I am really going to have to do it."

As we talked, I understood that indeed, his energy and his time were too limited for him to actually write out more of the faith and wisdom of his life story. Jim's realism took my hopes for preserving his voice in a different direction. The faith and courage that he was living before my eyes gave me a new idea. "What if I help you with the writing?" I asked him. "What if you tell me what you want to say and I find a way to write it down?"

"Hey," he answered, "that would be really great."

And so we made a simple and sacred arrangement — he would give me his papers and talk to me about them, and I would listen and somehow, someday, put his wisdom into words. Jim promised to go through his papers and find the outlines and paragraphs that he wanted included in his life story. He thought that he should sort that material out before he went to live at St. Teresa's, the Maryknoll Fathers and Brothers nursing home. As he stood to leave my office he said, "This will be a great relief for me. But don't kill yourself trying to get it done." I laughed at his familiar warning. Jim had always thought that I work too hard and could benefit from contemplating the AA slogans "Easy Does It" and "First Things First."

At that time, I was inclined to listen to him. My attention was being drawn in a number of different directions, some of them more threatening than others. Besides my struggle with my own illness, my husband had recently gone through eye surgery. Difficult interpersonal situations were teaching me that of all the deadly sins, I seem to like anger and pride the best. I was humbled to discover how proficient I was at both. There was plenty that I was trying to learn to live with, often through less than gentle measures. I was very tired and wondered if I had spoken too quickly in offering to put Jim's ideas into words.

It would take most of the summer for me to realize that I had not simply taken on a task to be completed. Rather, I had been invited into a journey of healing that took place in the context of Jim Lenihan's dying. Jim was asking me to be the guardian of his lessons not just in the written word, but in my own soul.

It was a few weeks before Jim and I started to converse about the autobiography and outlines. First he estimated how quickly his strength was waning and decided that he wanted to make one more trip while he could still travel. He wanted to swim in the ocean and visit a casino before he died. He called me when he returned from the trip and said that he had had a wonderful swim. He had also done well in the casino, hitting a slot machine jackpot on the first try. "So there I was, a dying man catching the quarters from a slot machine. I thought that was proof that God has a pretty good sense of humor." And with that we began the series of conversations in which Jim generously put flesh on the bones of his outlines and autobiography.

Early in the process, Jim gave me two letters. The first was to a Maryknoll colleague stating that we were working together on the papers and that he was giving me permission to continue the work after his death. The second was a copy of a letter he had written to the general leadership of Maryknoll some seventeen years earlier. The letter stated:

If I am sober at the time of my death, I request that it be made public that I was an alcoholic in recovery. The basic reason for this request is that it may contribute to reducing a common misconception and help those still living to realize that alcoholism is a chronic illness which is treatable and can be arrested.

The purpose of showing me these letters was to make it clear that Jim wanted the story told "straight." The depth of Jim's learning through life, the wisdom that speaks to the heart of life's meaning, had been hard won. He wanted the legacy of his life to be hope. All of us must deal with something that taxes the soul. For Jim, alcoholism was a metaphor for the reality of human life — sooner or later we must all surrender to a higher power.

Thus began what would prove to be the extraordinary summer of 1998. Over the course of warm, humid days and rain that brought the Hudson Valley into full growth, Jim and I met in his room at St. Teresa's. We talked about his life experience, his hopes, his dreams, his understandings. We talked about his death and the process of his dying. We talked about my illness and one day even compared notes on medications and their side effects. Looking at the work done earlier in his life allowed Jim to integrate the deeper meaning of his experience. This integration happened in slices of life — stories of the missions in Africa, AA meetings, quiet prayers. Listening to him taught me about "living through" something as a sacred calling that requires surrender more than personal strength. I learned from him the difference between being healed and being cured. With some relief, I learned that as long as we are human we are both unfinished and deeply loved.

Jim's failing health was quite visible through the process of our conversations. First he needed to stay in a wheelchair and then in his bed, and long before I was ready, he could not speak. I continued to visit him. The last time I sat by his bed, Jim's sister Theresa and her husband, Ed, were there, reading Jim the gospel of the day. Theresa had found more papers and followed Jim's instruction to give them to me. Reduced to the essence of his goodness, he had become more spirit than flesh. Two days later, he died.

For two and a half years, I had the autobiography and outlines gathered in one place by my desk. At first I was too sad to put the material together, then I was too sick, and then I was too task oriented. I wanted to tell his story, and only his story, in a linear way. I tried moving around paragraphs and turning outlines into sentences. The result was absent of life. Finally I realized that the only way I could begin to do justice to the material Jim left me is by telling

9

the story as he unfolded it. That means that I had to cycle through the themes of Jim's story as we all must cycle through our particular life challenges. I needed to revisit that special summer with a willingness to again be changed by it. To do that has meant praying as well as editing, telling the story of Jim's profound impact on me as well as putting forth the general principles he knew so well. It has meant over and over again confronting my own sadness, hesitancy, and denial of life's realities. It has both stirred me up and calmed me down, always feeling like holy work.

What Jim left for me to do was to integrate the meaning of his words into my own ongoing journey, to live with his story and my own limitations, to do my best and let God handle the rest. That has been a transforming experience for me. Since he died, I have felt Jim speaking deeply to my life through the notes that he left in my care. I have felt him alive in this process, a touchstone when I would let life lead me into grandiosity or depression. I have felt Jim nudging me in the process as words like "keep it simple" and "let it go and let God" come gently to mind.

Ultimately, this is a story about faith. Such stories are always heard most deeply through the filter of a personal experience. For Jim, the process of dying was an opportunity to celebrate the reality of rebirth. My own dying and the rebirth were — and are — richly blessed by having listened to Jim. It is a great pleasure to celebrate Jim's gift of hope. At the same time, this is a dangerous undertaking. It is tempting either to reduce the material too neatly or to write the story with too much detachment. At best I can draw a reflective sketch of the man who lived a very rich life. But sometimes the sketch is better because its form admits that reality cannot be adequately reproduced on the page. What appears in these lines are themes and shadows that suggest much more — a life given expression within the empty spaces of Jim's outlines. This is not an exhaustive biography, nor is it meant to be. Present in these pages are the themes that Jim talked about as he reviewed his life. As Jim's longtime friend Father Ed Killackey said, "He lived his life in outlines, not paragraphs. He was always looking ahead at the next thing he needed to do." I have done my best to fill in the outline while honoring Jim's intentions in the story he told to me and to himself in the last days of his life.

It is my hope and my deepest prayer that these pages reveal that acceptance of the presence and love of God is not only a fundamental step on the spiritual journey; it is the legacy of Jim Lenihan's life. It is also the way in which I follow Jim's advice and the AA wisdom to keep both of our stories green lest we forget the great miracles that God has done — in life, in death, and in life revealed again. My relationship with Jim Lenihan was one such miracle.

# *Tentative Meetings*

T HE FIRST TIME that I met Jim I really did not want to be in his presence. I had agreed to the original idea of inviting Jim to speak to our pastoral team about alcoholism and its effect on families largely because I didn't want to appear to be a coward. I certainly did not want to admit that I thought I already knew everything I needed to know about alcoholism, thank you, and I was not in need of further education, especially about the impact of alcoholism on family members. I had read a bit on that topic and actually felt kind of sorry for those people that it described; clearly I was not affected in any significant way — that I admitted — by the alcoholism of others. I could not express any of these ideas because I liked to believe I was open to growth. What mattered most in my mind was a long-ago decision that I would never be an alcoholic. I didn't drink, and as far as I was concerned, there was not much more that I needed to know.

When we arrived at the office the morning of the workshop, I felt like making conversation over coffee was going to be a major stretch. I was on maternity leave with my second child and cowardice was running high. The baby was five weeks old and not yet sleeping through the night; his two-and-a-half-year-old brother was still not quite accepting the interloper in the crib. Feeling rested or intellectually curious were things of memory. I was living the isolation of a period defined by night feedings, Sesame Street, and the exhaustion that narrows the borders of the newborn world. I really did not want to come in to the office for a workshop about alcoholism led by a priest I had never met. I frankly felt too tired to engage with someone new, particularly about a topic where the callus of my hesitation and denial had formed over very tender skin.

My mind was preoccupied with when to feed the baby that I had in tow and how my other son was doing with the babysitter. Jim's friendliness broke through my hesitation as he shook my hand. With short, salt-and-pepper gray hair, Jim looked at the baby as his bright blue eyes lit up his long, thin face. While gently putting his finger in the baby's hand Jim said, "How old is this little laddie?" Jim told me that he was very happy that I could make it that day. I felt his sincerity and honesty. I also perceived that Jim was absolutely present to our conversation. It mattered to him that I was there. He said that he knew the baby had needs and encouraged me to respond to him whenever I needed during the talk. "I won't be offended if you get up and leave," he said. I found that a huge relief and was hoping to leave the room often.

I sat and listened to Jim's talk, holding the baby as he slept and stepping out of the room when he awoke. I heard some of Jim's material as I walked and rocked the baby in the hallway; some of it I missed altogether. I heard Jim say that alcoholism is a disease that is not chosen by the alcoholic. While I intellectually knew and understood that concept, I had never been able to fully absorb it into my skin. The reality that alcoholics and their families often live in total isolation, unaware of the prevalence of the disease or the possibilities of recovery, is part of the vicious cycle of the disease. At some point, I had made a decision that I would never be afflicted with alcoholism, and I seriously believed that it was my will that made it so. As Jim spoke, recognition of vulnerability to alcoholism and to life stirred in my soul. At the end of the afternoon, my ability to re-call or repeat exactly what Jim had presented was patchy, at best. Nonetheless, I was impressed on a level I could not quite explain. I remembered the day in a way that was very alive — the feel of the baby resting on my shoulder, the sense that Jim Lenihan was a gentle, honest man who truly was as he ap-peared to be. I recognized him as a man who had no time for denial. Something within him expected and demanded that he do nothing less than tell the truth to himself and to others. I understand much better now that what stirred in me that day was an inkling — nothing more — that I was ready to learn something that Jim Lenihan could teach me. But not that afternoon, and definitely not all at once.

I did not see Jim again until several years later when Jim and I had become co-workers on a personnel team. Jim worked with alcoholism assessment; I worked with overall administration and individual counseling. My children were older, though early in the morning we still watched *Sesame Street,* and occasionally sleepless nights left me numb. I had gone to graduate school in counseling but, as is often the case, had not done a thorough study of alcoholism. I knew that Jim could help me learn more about alcoholism through his personal knowledge that responded to rising questions in my heart. I needed help working with others in counseling and spiritual direction. Nonetheless, I hesitated when I called Jim to set up a meeting. I knew deep down that if I was going to work with Jim, I was going to be called to honesty about what all of this learning meant to me personally. I thought that he was likely to ask me what I was doing to bring the knowledge into my own life and be changed by it. And eventually, he did.

But in the first phone conversation he had to catch up on things like "How is your baby?" and "How did you like your studies?" Jim was very friendly in our exchange, expressing a confidence in me that I did not feel. "You'll do fine," he told me. "We'll talk more about that." The next day he walked over to my office wearing sunglasses and a trademark sailor's hat that kept the rays from further injuring his eyes or his skin. "I can't face the doctor if I get skin cancer again," he said as he threw his hat in the chair. "I'm paying the price for my youth in the sun." Jim was delighted to become my mentor in working with people suffering from chemical dependency. "It can drive you crazy," he said, "but working with chemically dependent people is the most rewarding work on earth. It keeps you honest." I didn't have the heart to tell him that being kept honest was what I was afraid of. I did not want to admit that I was afraid of exploring alcoholism and all of its human realities. Learning more might expose within me a heart of flesh.

Through his own experience and study, Jim drew from a deep well of understanding about chemical dependency and about life. Jim told me that he wanted me to grasp the meaning of recovery at the most fundamental and heart-felt level. He wanted me to understand about the desperation and the miracles. Conversations with Jim about alcoholism were testimonies about spirituality, vitality, and renewal. I asked questions, and he gave me ideas that were direct and without qualification. Jim taught me what I didn't learn in school. He taught me that ideas and concepts are much less tidy when experienced through human life and feeling. Jim had an appreciation for theory and ideas but he believed that it was not the theory that made people better. "I don't want to hear about somebody's ideas about alcoholism," he told me. "I want them to be able to tell me about their experience." He had fully integrated the program slogan to "keep it simple." I, on the other hand, suffered a need to keep it all very complicated and as far away from myself as possible. Further, I was afraid to ask people questions in counseling that were related to drinking. I said — and perhaps at that time truly believed — that I did not want to bring alcoholism up with people because I thought that it might seem judgmental to do so. Obviously I still deep down viewed alcoholism as some kind of personal failure. If not, why would there be judgment on my mind?

One day after I knew that I had missed some obvious clues with a client, I asked Jim how to talk to people about their drinking. "That's easy," he answered. "You ask them. Directly, gently, and without judgment. You just say to them, 'Now let's talk a bit about your drinking.' Listen to what the person says and offer feedback. You don't have to make the diagnosis, but you do have to ask. They may have a life-threatening disease, after all. What are you going to do? Let them die because it makes you nervous?"

Jim gave me books and papers to read as background. Intuiting that it was not so much a fear of passing judgment but a few ghosts of my experience circling around me, Jim added, "But what you really need to do," he said, "is get yourself to some open AA meetings and witness how the program gives people their lives back." I must have looked hesitant or quizzical at that suggestion because Jim looked me straight in the eye and said, "What's wrong? Are you afraid you might learn something?"

I went to the open meetings, and I did learn something. The first thing that I discovered was that I desperately wanted to be wearing a name tag that said "I am not an alcoholic." I did judge alcoholism harshly, and I wanted to be sure that people understood that it was not *my* problem. Like most people who have witnessed or experienced the pain caused by the alcoholism of someone else, I was determined that I would never develop the disease. I wanted to be sure that other people didn't mistakenly assume that I had. The right theories and understandings aside, I still believed that alcoholism was a matter of will and personal determination. I was proud that, in fact, alcoholism had not happened to me. I did not want to be confused with someone who had not been as lucky.

Like most people walking through the doors of an AA or Alanon meeting for the first time, I could not understand the sound of laughter coming from the room. How could there be joy among people suffering from such a difficult disease? For a moment, it actually felt insulting. I was walking up the stairs to the meeting nervous and newly aware of my feelings, and the people at the AA meeting (or, in my mind at the moment, the people who cause such suffering for others) all seemed to be having a good time. It was difficult to hold on to my pride in that atmosphere. Listening to people over a period of weeks, it became apparent to me that the source of joy was not the illness but the spirit of ongoing recovery from it. I realized through the AA meetings that Jim was part of a larger group of people that talked about alcoholism in the same way. I saw that the descriptions, symptoms, and statistics in the books are lived out over and over again in human suffering and sorrow. I learned that alcoholism is a disease that, untreated, leads to insanity and death. I began to understand that having a disease is very different from a lack of will. For all of the pain it causes, alcoholism is not chosen. To recover from alcoholism is a powerful choice made over and over again in the course of the day.

The stories and relationships of AA had great meaning for me because they opened up a space for forgiveness of others by forgiving my own helplessness in overpowering situations.

I shared with Jim that I was finding the AA meetings helpful.

"To stand before the meeting and say, 'I am an alcoholic' is my lifeline," he told me. "It reminds us of who we are and how we must turn ourselves over to God."

Jim thought it was wonderful whenever people were traveling through some uncharted territory in their own soul. "You need to know who you are and where you come from if you are going to be authentic with other people and before God. You have to keep your story green." Keeping the story green means that it is fresh in your mind, never far from current experience, never "in the past." At the same time, the AA model teaches that human suffering is meant to be transformative, not isolating. Through Jim's guidance, I began to see just how deep that transformation can be.

Jim and I worked together for three years. On the surface, we could not have been more different. I grew up in Iowa; he was born in Brooklyn. Jim was ordained to the priesthood the year that I was born. While Jim was focusing on the concerns of retirement, I was juggling family and work. Yet there was something that we each respected in the other, and while I couldn't identify it at the time, I believe that we both had plenty of experience in finding joy through the embrace of limitation.

At the age of seventy Jim decided to accept an invitation from a classmate to be "actively retired" in American Samoa. We did not keep in touch, yet I always thought of Jim in a warm way. I had no way of knowing that the next time I saw Jim, it would be at the end of his life. And as he later wrote, neither did he.

*The cancer diagnosis was a surprise. First the x-ray showed tumors in my lungs. Further studies in New York showed that the cancer had spread to the spinal column. I had a series of twelve radiation treatments that ended on Good Friday, no less. Surrendering to the effects of the radiation, I knew that I had to continue to let God be in charge of my life. My family, friends, and colleagues supported my decision to accept no further treatment. I had pretty much made that decision during what I now call my "Las Vegas Retreat."*

*On the way from Samoa to New York, I needed to make a stop in the western United States to break up the trip. I decided to stop in Las Vegas because I had never been there before and I was catching on that I probably wouldn't have an opportunity to be there again. It made sense to rest in a city I had never been to before because I'd never been terminally ill before either. I thought that the two things went together. I walked around and looked at the sights and rested when I needed to. I started to slow down and accept the reality that I had contracted cancer, and that my life was going to end pretty soon. I told God, "You are going to have to help me with this because I've never physically died before and I really don't know how to do it." From that moment, I felt a slowing down inside me that brought me to a moment of inner peace. I was completely at ease with myself and with God's loving care in my cancer. I realized that dying is a lot like living — all that you can do is be with the present moment and count on God teaching you what you need to know. Using energy from God, I came to accept my medical condition and to journey through the moment.*

For Jim to learn what he needed to know for the end of his life, he turned back to the beginnings and the middles that had formed him and taught him the constancy of God's care. What he found there only deepened his trust in God's presence through the whole of his life. Through the grace of God, he succeeded in sharing that presence with more people than he ever knew.

# THREE

# Mission St. Teresa's

WHEN I FIRST visited Jim's room at Mission St. Teresa's, the nursing care center for Maryknoll Fathers and Brothers, I was surprised at how much the room already looked like Jim. He sat in a chair next to his bed. Jim's prayer books and AA literature were neatly stacked on a nearby table, easily within reach. Jim had hung a few family pictures on the wall, including one taken of him when he was on the deck of a merchant marine vessel. He was caught in the shadows in the picture, the profile of a young man looking out to sea somehow bearing witness to a different passage. A colorful afghan lay across the foot of the hospital bed.

"Come on in and pull up a chair," Jim said, "and welcome to my new home." Jim beckoned me to the window. "Before you sit down come over here and see the million dollar view." Outside Jim's window lay an open field and the hills and lush trees of the Hudson Valley. Jim enjoyed seeing summer at its peak as well as watching the families of deer that ran across the field. "I couldn't ask for a better view of the world," Jim said.

Before I sat down, Jim asked me, "So did you read the article on Irish American families?" I had indeed read the article, which was actually a chapter from a book about the impact of ethnicity on family systems. "I found it fascinating," I said. Jim wanted to make certain that I understood that "we're all bigger than our immediate relatives." I assured Jim that I understood that idea very well. "Good," he replied, "because we can't talk about the Lenihans if you don't know about the Irish and their families. And we can't talk about the Irish if we don't talk about everyone else. What I learned in Africa is that we are all part of everyone else's history. By the way, McGee is your married name. What's your family background?" I told him about my extended Irish family and my paternal British grandfather who, until the day he died in 1968, referred to the United States as the colonies. Jim chuckled and observed that between my genetic roots and having carefully done the required reading, I was prepared to listen to him speak about the Lenihans. I felt ready to go with him into the story where the whole world enters the tiny rooms of childhood memory, expanding them until we know ourselves as whole.

There are within the chambers of every family's heart deep sorrows, great unspoken secrets, unanswered questions, and threads of history that when pulled unravel the cloak of perception. It is in the unraveling that truth is known and rewoven into adult understanding. When Jim began the work of pulling and weaving, he had lived more than seventy years. He had traveled the world, lived for more than three decades in a culture and language worlds apart from his Long Island home. Through his alcoholism Jim had embraced his humanity, and he began the process of working on his family history prepared to hold close and love whatever was found there. Within the history he found celebrated family stories and a few mysteries and dead ends, lost children and very sad deaths, diseases of the body and soul that tore relationships apart. He understood those events as part of his own history and life. To Jim his family history was living, documented in baptismal certificates and gravestones, the history of Ireland and the United States, a context of earlier lives and formative events that reached across four generations. The history became a key to understanding life choices and sacrifices, as well as sources of joy and fulfillment.

Jim was reared in a big house on Long Island, the sixth of nine children — five girls (Frances, Gertrude, Clair, Betty, Theresa) and four boys (Bernard, James, Edward, and Paul) — born to Bernard and Irene

Colligan Lenihan between 1916 and 1930. Family legend holds that Bernard was visiting a sick friend in the hospital when he met a nurse named Irene in 1914. Both Irene and Jim had remnants of the Irish famine in their bloodline. Grandparents on all sides had left barren fields and emigrated to New York City in search of abundance to replace fear and scarcity. Irene and Bernard were born into that struggle to build a new life far removed from the threat of starvation. However, as is so often the human experience, the reverberation of the first crossings carried over into other sorrows that intervened in the lives of both families. There were problems with alcoholism in Irene's family, and a strain of depression ran deep in Bernard's, afflicting and hospitalizing his younger brother for life. "They never spoke of it though," Jim told me with a laugh. "You know that's the Irish way of dealing with a family crisis."

Throughout her life, Irene was devoted to her mother. When rendered blind in old age, Irene's mother remained independent, living in a home adjacent to the Lenihan children's Catholic school. Each of the siblings took turns visiting Grandma at lunchtime. She made her grandchildren sandwiches by touch. As a child, Jim considered visiting his grandmother to be an obligation. When he learned more about her life and family history, Jim had profound appreciation for the grandmother who lived alone next to the church. Suffering and adversity seem to have bred courage and independence into the blood and bones of Colligan women and their descendants. Over the course of his life, Jim became deeply grateful for the courage his mother's family had shown, and he came to embody it. As a child, however, it was sometimes difficult to fully appreciate that strength because Jim had simply always known it as part of life.

Irene was a tall, graceful, and beautiful woman with many interests and a great love of Irish music. She worked very hard to attend nursing school, and then in her work as a nurse. Though she gave up nursing when she married, Irene returned to work in a Long Island hospital when World War II created a pressing need for nurses on the home front. Whether working outside the home or not, Irene always carried with her the gentle touch and calm spirit of nursing. Her skills served her well in managing a household with nine active children. Throughout her life, Irene's favorite expressions were those whispers of Ireland that when spoken on the exhaled breath become a cross between any emotion — from frustration to wonderment — and a quick prayer. "Jesus, Mary, and Joseph" and "Mother of God" punctuated her daily speech. Because the words could mean almost anything, they had enormous potential for communicating feelings that might otherwise be too difficult to put into words.

Bernard was born and baptized in Manhattan in the Church of St. Gabriel in 1888. Named for the archangel, the church did not survive the progress of New York City and was torn down to make way for the Queens-Midtown tunnel. The baptismal records of the church were moved to the nearby Church of the Sacred Heart — the transition of record and memory so complete that those passing through the tunnel today have no way of knowing that its entrance was built over the threshold of the archangel's church. Bernard never finished grammar school. Instead he worked for the moving company that his father founded and personally built into a strong business. Eventually he stopped working for his father's company and labored on behalf a competitor. The story behind that career change was never fully known, though Jim thought it safe to assume that there had been some sort of rift between his father and grandfather — if not before then after his father went to work for the competition. This untold story led Jim to observe, "It was just another one of those things that no one talked about but everyone knew." Hearing descriptions of his paternal grandfather, Jim suspected that his father needed to be independent and out from under the control of a man who could be very harsh and demanding.

Bernard went on to found his own business, the Franklin Fireproof Warehouse in Brooklyn. Since he was opening a business that was in direct competition with his own father, Jim assumed over the silence that family relations were not strengthened by his father's decision. Bernard had not only turned his back on the family business; he had exceeded his father's success.

*I'm told that my grandfather was a very domineering man and that getting out from under his control was part of why my father wanted his own business. I don't know what my grandfather said or did when he found out about the new business, but I can't image he was happy, but again, we did not talk about that.*

The ancient story of the wounds between fathers and sons was hidden in the silence. Two generations from the famine, Bernard became a wealthy man. He was a tolerant and gentle person who wanted to be near his children. Jim said of Bernard, "He had a zest for living without being ostentatious. His interest and enthusiasm in life were high." Bernard brought tenderness to his children in stark contrast to his own domineering father.

*When I was seven or eight years old, I experienced leg cramps at night. Some nights it was very painful and it would awaken me. One night when I woke up, I was groaning and moaning just like a little boy, and my father came and applied Absorbine Junior to my legs. "Jim, do you want to grow up?" Of course I said that I did. He then told me that I was experiencing growing pains and that they were part of life. I never forgot that and it has served me well to remember that difficulties are an opportunity to "grow up a bit more." There is a big difference between becoming an adult and really growing up.*

Jim began to understand that distinction in the loving, middle-of-the-night care that his father offered him. Jim would refer to his father's wisdom on growing pains for the rest of his life. He also observed that it took him about fifty years from the time of his father's ministrations to seriously start growing up.

Bernard bought a 16mm camera to photograph moving jobs. That camera would become his means of documenting life, of leaving behind a story of the time he spent with his children and his vision of the world. It was a vision of kindness, enthusiasm for life, and a deep love of his children that was given face and shape in the moments his photographs preserved. "When I look at those photographs," Jim said, "I know how much he loved us." Jim treasured the memory of those photographs because they gave him a clear point of entry into his father's experience and view of the world.

Home was a warm and hospitable place for Jim. In the order of the day, Irene ran the home and Bernard ran the business. The girls worked in the house; the boys worked outside. The Lenihan house was the gathering place for the extended family on holidays and special occasions. Jim remembered the house as full of people but under control.

*On Sunday, as was our family custom, we all were expected to eat together in our family dining room. My mother did the cooking, sometimes making roast beef, which my father would then carve and distribute. This was one of the sacred times at home and it was rare that we were not all together. Other relatives visited and ate with us.*

Because Jim was thin and somewhat sickly, his mother always saved the juice from the meat and gave it to him to drink. Jim remembered feeling singled out and embarrassed by that act of care. When I remarked to Jim that those meals were a continuing of the Eucharist celebrated earlier in the day, he agreed. Body and blood then took on new perspective, and the years of swigging down beef juice felt more complete to Jim. "I get it now," he said, "but then it was just something that a kid didn't want to do. It's hard for kids to understand the love and concern of their parents." Particularly, Jim would note, if that love included things that tasted bad.

The communication of the Catholic faith was woven into daily life like the rituals of the family. This was a time when New Yorkers identified their neighborhoods by parish, not streets. For Catholics, the parish was the still point of the city map and no interpretation was necessary. The Lenihans knew themselves to be Catholic with the same certainty as they knew their Irish heritage. Their Catholicism was expressed in the rituals of grace before meals, a family rosary prayed after dinner, participation in weekly mass, and a worldview that believed in the grace of God. Being Catholic comforted them, gave them a sense of identity, and provided expression of the passages of life. There were no long discussions about being Catholic or questions about doctrine or practice. Catholicism was simply part of their being, like the shape of their faces or their surname, or the way the Lenihans ate their meals.

Bernard bought two summer homes, first one at the shore and later one in the country. Jim remembered the summer homes as places where life was carefree and cousins abounded as playmates. While Jim was working on the family history, he had conversations with his sister Theresa about her recollections of growing up on Long Island. She verified and shared Jim's memories of a household that was very hospitable and open. Theresa also remembered that there were no scapegoats or favorite children. There was a fairness and evenness in the way discipline was carried out. Most transgressions were handled with a withdrawal of privileges and a requisite amount of guilt.

Jim remembered only one serious confrontation with either one of his parents. When he was twelve, Jim was struck by Bernard after being caught smoking a cigar. Cigar smoking would become Jim's trademark as an adult and ultimately play a major role in his developing lung cancer. "Not all of our hang-ups are so obvious," Jim said to me wryly. "I guess I didn't get the message, or else I've been reacting to that slap all of my life." In either case, Jim identified the moment as an assertion — however misguided — of independence. And, as Jim pointed out, he really liked smoking cigars even though he knew all along that they held the potential to kill him. "My first independent decision," he said, "and it was a bad one."

Jim attended Catholic schools and in high school became a boxer. Because he weighed only 115 pounds, Irene objected to Jim's participation in boxing. As a nurse, she could vividly imagine the injuries that were possible for a slight boy participating in a rough sport. Bernard, however, had been a boxer in his youth, and he conspired with Jim to get him to a boxing match. Bernard threw the young boxer's gym bag from the third floor and put it in the car. He then told Irene that he was taking Jim to the movies. Perhaps the scheme would have gone unnoticed if Jim had not won the boxing match. His picture was printed the next day in the local newspaper, which laid the plot bare. Jim was grateful that day that his mother desperately disliked confrontation and conflict in the family. "Her fear served me well that day," he said, "though it was a bit of a problem for me later in life." Learning to speak up was to become the backbone of Jim's recovery from alcoholism.

Of all the silences in the family, the one that most haunted Jim was the story of Bernard's brother who lived in the Pilgrim State Mental Hospital. "I know that every Sunday my father went to visit his brother," Jim said. "I know that when he died at the hospital, my father went to the funeral. I know that he grieved. But it was silent in the family." The silence, as is so often the case, was supported by a sense of shame about alcoholism or mental illness. It would be years before Jim's own experience led him to understand the isolation caused by the perception that labeled such sorrows "failures of will."

Recent genetic research sheds some light on one of the reasons that Jim felt both haunted and curious about his uncle. The genetic marker for an inherited predisposition toward alcoholism and depression has been identified and studied. Research has scientifically documented what has been experientially known for generations. Alcoholism and depression both run in families. British researchers have discovered that the same gene that predicts a predisposition to alcoholism also predicts a tendency toward depression. Sometimes a person is afflicted only by depression or only by alcoholism. Some people drink to cover the pain of their depression; some people become depressed from the use of alcohol. The diseases are interwoven, and many people suffer from both.

No one yet knows why one disease or another becomes manifested in a person, but the recognition of the interrelationship of depression and alcoholism promises hope for future treatment. Both diseases are life-threatening, and often it is the shame of it that kills people. To Jim, that was the great sorrow of his uncle's death. Today, in spite of the fact that both diseases are effectively treatable, the shame lingers. And that, Jim said, is just plain wrong. As he told the story of his uncle's death, Jim wondered out loud how many people suffer and die needlessly because they fear the judgment of others. Jim brought no such judgment to the family history. He said instead, "There but for the grace of God go any of us." At the same time, he never ceased to wonder at the miracle that he had entered recovery from something as life-threatening as alcoholism. His uncle's depression was a close cousin to Jim's own illness, which made him appreciate the wonder of his own recovery even more.

At the time that Jim and I were having this conversation, I was well acquainted with — indeed haunted by — the reality of depression. I had by then struggled for some time with depression of my own. Whether predecessor or successor of my chronic physical illness I do not know. What is certain is that I suffered from shame and a feeling of weakness that I could not better control my own mood. I could barely accept that I had a physically measurable and visible disease. The experience of depression was something I could not initially understand at all, particularly when it refused to go away. With some hesitation, I admitted this reality as Jim and I talked about his uncle. My reluctance and difficulty in discussing the subject uncovered the truth that I had been as judgmental about my own depression as I had once been about other people's alcoholism. I considered my depression to be a personal failure of the worst kind, in no small part because I had not planned to be depressed, I didn't want to be depressed, and nonetheless the experience remains part of my life. The disease is impossible to control by willpower alone. The reality of depression in my life chipped away at the stubborn vestiges of pride that I had managed to escape alcoholism. My own vulnerability to a disease affecting the body and soul opened a new door for understanding and mercy upon others who suffered. That understanding unfolded gradually, however, and like the alcoholic, I tried to chase away my depression with good thoughts and resolutions. I did not seek effective treatment because I thought that medication and therapy were for people who were *really* sick. After all, I still functioned fairly well. I just needed to make a decision and stick with it. Thus, I "dodged the bullet" of understanding or help for far too long.

When I hesitantly told all of that to Jim, he said, "You sound just like a functional alcoholic." That statement initially took me by surprise and made me want to argue with him. Then I realized that the conversation about Jim's uncle was allowing me to admit my depression to another human being, much like what happens in the Twelve Steps of AA. Depression is as much a part of my life as alcoholism was part of Jim's. I could not miss our common journey when Jim asked me the same question I had heard him ask others, "So now that you know the problem, what are you doing about it?" I told him that I had done a lot about it, including counseling and searching out more information. Through research

I learned that 50 percent of people with rheumatoid arthritis at some point suffer from clinical depression and that there is a strong genetic predisposition for both diseases. My own experience led me to believe that the other 50 percent of arthritis patients under-reported their symptoms — and I quickly knew that if queried earlier, I would have fallen into that half. "Nothing I can't handle," I would have told anyone who asked. Depression is hell for the strong-willed.

Soon after reading the statistics on the rate of depression in people with arthritis and in the general population, I more or less backed into trying an antidepressant medication. My doctor suggested it as a way of counteracting the fact that, like many people with rheumatoid arthritis — and alcoholism and depression — I had great difficulty getting restful sleep. As long as the medication was being offered as treatment of the physical illness, I could take the antidepressants. After two weeks on the medication, I woke up one morning still feeling physical pain but without the mental fog that had come to feel so familiar. I told Jim that my first lucid thought in months was "I have been a fool about not getting help and taking medication." And with that Jim said, "You're finally getting the idea. I'm happy for you."

Actually controlling depression requires as much attention as any other disease. It would take another step for me to realize and respect the delicacy of the chemistry and the ways in which I could contribute to my own sense of well-being through exercise, meditation, and other habits of living. It would take even more time to incorporate what I had learned about alcoholism into my own quiet — and isolating — experience of depression. Integrating the learning was much easier when I framed it within the reality of someone else's disease. To claim it for myself began as Jim and I talked about his uncle's hidden depression.

Over time, one of the most enduring gifts of my relationship with Jim — especially in his last months of life and the years of reflection that have followed — has come through embracing the reality that disease and recovery are part of life and its renewal. Knowing that we suffered such related diseases opened up new possibilities for healing through the knowledge that God does not mean for us to suffer alone. Sooner or later, the whole world comes to join us in experiences that shatter perceptions and initially break our hearts. Only then do we really know ourselves both as whole people and families at the fundamental levels of life. Jim, his uncle, and I carried the same marker gene and, at a level sometimes hidden from the world, the same zest for life.

## FOUR

# *Goods at Sea*

J IM GRADUATED from high school in the middle
of World War II. Everyone in the country was
responding to the pressing needs of the war. Ra-
tioning their daily use of goods, hearing news about
the deaths of young men, and participating in blackouts kept the reality of the war near at hand. Jim's
mother went back to work as a maternity nurse to
free a younger woman for the Army Nursing Corps.
There was no question that a young, healthy man
graduating from high school would participate directly in the war effort through military service of
some kind.

Jim left home in 1943 and entered the U.S. Merchant Marine Academy at Kings Point, New York.
After graduation from the academy, Jim immediately
went to work at sea. Before leaving, he told the young
woman that he was dating that she should feel free
to date other men while he was gone. "I thought that
was only fair," he said, "since I was going off to the
war zone." Jim did not see her again.

Jim sailed the world with the merchant marines,

carrying cargo and troops for the war effort. The merchant marines did very dangerous work. The personnel troops and supplies that the ships carried were vital for the war. The importance of their mission made the convoys of ships the target of torpedo and bomb attacks. Jim witnessed nearby ships blow up and sink; at one point in the war, 30 to 40 percent of merchant marine ships did not return to their point of origin; a total of 820 ships were lost by the end of the war. Though technically civilians, the merchant marines had the highest loss ratio of any service in the war — 1 in 32 were killed. More than 11,000 of the 250,000 men serving were left wounded, many with permanent injuries.

Jim credited his youth with saving him from a paralyzing fear of death during the war. Serving in the merchant marines, however, led Jim to an experience of vulnerability that he had not known earlier. The vulnerability led to a deepening of his faith that in many ways set a pattern for his adult life. Though he saw destruction around him and experienced some dramatic near misses, Jim came to believe that "God was not finished with me yet and only God could decide when it was my time to die." In spite of the danger, Jim fell in love with the sea and sailing; he became a second mate by the end of the war.

There were, however, great losses during the war, of people he knew, of the way of life he knew as a child, of his sense of home. Jim read and appreciated his father's newsy letters that described the lives of his siblings and events around the Lenihan home. Yet even the warmth of the letters provoked a certain emptiness in him. "Once I went to the war," he said, "I never lived at my family home again as a young man. After I left, my mother stored all of my things in the attic, tucked away, I think so she wouldn't be so afraid. When the war ended, I had become an adult. I didn't know that would happen when I left, and it gave me an empty feeling when I returned."

As civilians, the merchant marines were sometimes looked down upon by men serving in the armed forces, in part because of the sailors' independence about choosing their assignments. If his ship went down, however, the merchant marine was on his own to find a ride home. Generally this was accomplished through taking a berth on another ship, sometimes paying for the return voyage. The merchant marines were not recognized as veterans until fifty years after the war ended. Thus when Jim returned, he was excluded from many of the benefits that helped other veterans get reestablished after the war. Jim carried a lingering sense of being "second best" because he had been a merchant marine. This was particularly true in the presence of veterans who had no difficulty reminding him that he had gone through the war as a "civilian."

Regardless of that criticism or any feelings arising from it, the experience at sea shaped Jim for the rest of his life. When he lived in Africa, other missioners would call him "a mariner trapped in the desert." Jim brought the bell from his last ship to Tanzania and hung it in the kitchen. The specificity of roles on the ship taught Jim a great deal about delegating authority and knowing his place in a larger order. That understanding helped him to empower others when he became a missionary priest.

As it did for many men of his generation, the war divided Jim's life into distinct before and after periods that were marked by upheaval, loss, and a renewed search for meaning. "The war years certainly made me begin to think of what was really important in life." Jim identified faith, service, and meaningful work as priorities. He was not sure, however, what that would concretely mean in his life. He attended Mount St. Mary's College, a small school tucked away in the hills of Emmitsburg, Maryland. Jim participated in the religious life of the campus. He was not sure exactly what he wanted to study or dedicate his life to, but he held firm to the important values he identified in the war. Finding his life's calling was an important and painful part of the process of growing up — and growing into who he was meant to be. And while he studied hard, Jim had no idea where to go next in life.

"When did you know that you wanted to be a priest?" I asked Jim.

"I guess it was quite a while after God knew," Jim answered. "I didn't consult anyone about where I was going to college, or what I was going to do. I didn't pray about it, never talked to my family or friends. I just set off in my independent way, doing what I thought was right. The beginning of Jim's plan. It never even occurred to me that God might have an idea for my life — even after surviving the war and believing that God had a purpose for my life."

Discerning one's vocation is often a process filled with mystery, false starts, confusion, and the desire for a quick conclusion and comfortable answers. Whatever form it takes, a true vocation is discovered in the claiming of one's own deepest gifts and desires in relationship to the wounds of the world. Individuals can be remarkably blind about their truest selves, a fact that Jim commented upon often. It is for that reason that God relies on the human community to identify gifts and longings in others. A call from God may be experienced directly by an individual, but as often as not directions appear through the human voice of someone who sees the gifts and cannot let them go by unnoticed. Often these clarifications take a person by surprise and are dismissed, at least temporarily. It takes courage to live into the defining elements of one's self. At the same time, when a real gift is identified, the longing to live it out becomes an energy that cannot be ignored.

Sometimes the call to a particular life comes from unexpected or underestimated sources. So it was with Jim. A classmate identified the gift when out of nowhere he asked Jim, "Have you ever thought about becoming a priest?" Jim laughed out loud and proclaimed, "No, I have not" — as if driving the idea out of his friend's mind would make the possibility flee from his own life. He got a big kick out of the question, but for months he gave the idea no conscious thought.

Since he did not have the GI bill to help him finance his college education, Jim was always looking for opportunities to make money for school. During the summer of 1947, the first summer after his freshman year, Jim took a berth on a ship and went back to work as a merchant marine. Initially, he was far more concerned about the immediacy of making money for the tuition than he was about discerning his vocation. Jim checked out an armload of books from the school library to carry him through his off hours. Most of the books turned out to be written by Christian authors who were quite clear in their poetic descriptions of the call from God. Among the works Jim read was the English poet Francis Thompson's "Hound of Heaven." Like Dorothy Day, Jim found Thompson's poetry to echo the longings in his own soul and his profound desire to run away from all that God was doing within him. Jim frequently quoted Thompson, particularly in relationship to the ongoing nature of his vocation:

I fled him down the nights and down the days.
I fled him down the labyrinthine ways of my
    own mind.

Jim began to realize that we do not control the mission of our lives so much as we allow a love beyond description to express itself in the gifts of our lives. Until the point in his life when he could no longer speak, Jim was expressing gratitude for that gift. He also remained conscious that answering his vocational questions did not free him of the desire to flee from God's love. Alcoholism had taught him much about the labyrinthine ways of the mind.

Looking back on that summer of spiritual awakening from the perspective of decades of priesthood, Jim pointed out the scriptural consistency of human beings trying to hide from the face of the living God. The theme of avoiding the call of God is seen in the Hebrew Scriptures, in the conversion of Paul, and in our own struggles with understanding God's will. Jim said, "We are made to love and be loved. To give and receive love is the calling and greatness of human beings. When we offer excuses about why we cannot hear the call of love, God responds 'Yes, I know,' and then calls us anyway." And for my benefit he added, "Remember that for some of us, the worst desolation is between our ears." Jim had long since learned not to put too much faith in the labyrinthine ways of the mind, and he recommended that I do the same. Make peace with wanting to flee, he suggested, and then stand still. Reason isn't everything.

The sea always led Jim to a spirit of contemplation and stillness. He reflected on his reading and let the idea of the priesthood take root in his heart. He asked God for guidance, and he began to feel a little bit less in control of his life. He experienced a deepening of his prayer that summer. While sailing during the war, Jim had consistently prayed for survival. Now he prayed at sea for direction, for right use of his talents, and for peace within a longing almost too deep to be named. Jim later wrote about the sense of call from God:

*We are called to do things that are difficult, tasks that we often really do not want to do. But God is persistent. As related in the Acts of the Apostles, Paul was thrown to the ground on the road to Damascus. It was a call from God to change his life, his way of thinking. God almost has to kick him on the head to get his attention. The call to Peter, James, and*

*John also came in a dramatic way on Mount Tabor. That our call comes in ordinary ways makes it no less urgent or authentic. God demands an answer.*

As Jim grew in his life, he began to understand that the call he felt at sea was only the beginning of a lifelong desire to be faithful to God's will. Slowly Jim was coming to understand that the most fundamental element of that call was fully accepting the presence of God's love. He would be guided by that unfolding presence until he died, at some moments with more appreciation than at others.

One of the ports of call that summer was Dar es Salaam in the country then called Tanganyika. It is unlikely that Jim knew when he sailed into that port what an important place Tanganyika would have in his life's mission. He certainly could never have imagined that he would be in that country for its transformation into the independent country of Tanzania, that he would know the president of the new republic, or that he would live there for thirty-seven years. During the summer, it was just one more stop on a long, long journey — a place that Jim glimpsed before going back to sea, a step along the way of earning money for tuition. By the end of the summer, Jim's experience of the presence of God overshadowed more practical goals, and he began to yearn for a means of giving shape to his longings. He began to seriously think about becoming a priest, and he wanted to make a decision as quickly as possible.

The patience that Jim developed on the ocean — and given his personality that was minimal — evaporated in September. When he returned to college, Jim wanted clarification about his future life on land, and he wanted it immediately. With the urgency of a man who had once seen ships blow up around him, Jim went to see the college chaplain. He was hoping that the chaplain would have some clever way of knowing whether or not Jim should become a priest. "I hoped that the chaplain would tell me what to do," Jim wrote. But the chaplain told him to continue to pray, a response that Jim found decidedly disappointing. Jim had learned to watch and wait on the sea; it was a totally different journey to do so in regard to his own life.

One of the key tools of Jim's later life was the use of three questions when facing an important life decision. Do I want to do this? Can I do this? Should I do this? Lacking those clarifying questions — and the profound recovery process that gave them meaning — Jim floated along impatiently in his life. He wanted to know what to do with his life, and he wanted to know it so that he could get on with implementing the plan. God's plan. Jim's plan. Jim needed to move on with life.

Becoming a priest was a possibility that many young Catholic men were contemplating in the wake of their war experience. The losses of the war had made men like Jim receptive to the deeper longings in their souls. They had confronted life and death in a way that usually occurs later in life. They desperately sought meaning in the terrible images they carried within themselves. The veterans of the war saw too much of life and death too soon. Many of those who survived carried a sense of mission; the war had spared them for a reason, and that reason was to make a contribution to life. Eventually these men would make up the largest classes in the history of American seminaries. For Jim, the war experience had an additional impact: he had literally seen the world, and he could no longer envision his life as contained on Long Island. He wanted to stretch beyond what he knew. As he waited and prayed and tried to follow the chaplain's advice, it became apparent to him that his vocation was to the foreign missions. "I could not explain why I said this to myself," he said. "I just knew it." Near the end of his life Jim wrote:

*Discernment is an art, an acquired skill which we learn by experience. It involves bringing all our problems and decisions to God in order to discover in prayer what God wishes us to do. This means be-*

*ing able to come to a listening quiet, surfacing the
concerns of the moment, handing them over to God
for guidance, and then waiting patiently for God to
show his will. We know that God always speaks in
peace and that turmoil or restlessness or a sense of
crisis are never his voice. At every stage of our life,
the fundamental, bedrock attitude must be "that the
One who began this good work in us will see that
it is finished when the Day of Christ Jesus comes"
(Philippians 1:6). All is God's work. That was Jesus'
way — and it must be ours too.*

Living into the silence that nurtured discernment
became an integral and defining element of Jim's vocation. Jim was to become a very astute helper to
others who were considering their life calling. But he
did not yet know that dimension of himself in the
fall of 1948. All he knew then was that his desire to
be a missionary priest felt peaceful in his soul. That
peace was a great relief for Jim in that it felt right
and it ended his ambiguity.

Having found his peace, Jim was ready to put the
plan in motion. When he went home at Christmas
and told his parents that he had decided to become
a missionary priest, his father was supportive and
his mother was surprised. "She thought that I was
kind of a rebel in my younger years," Jim explained.
After the initial shock wore off, however, his mother

was also supportive of Jim's decision. He returned to college not quite sure about the practical steps he needed to take to pursue his vocation. During the cold days of January, Jim's father sent him a book about Maryknoll. A family connection to Maryknoll reached back to his paternal grandmother who had bequeathed $250 to Maryknoll in its early years. Jim quickly came to believe that his vocation and Maryknoll were closely interrelated. He applied to the seminary and was accepted.

Jim's early years in the seminary foreshadowed not only his meaningful life as a missionary priest, but the disease that first would enslave him and then lead him to rebirth.

*The novitiate followed my two years of philosophy at Maryknoll in New York. Our novitiate was then located in Bedford, Massachusetts, in what had once been a farm. I believed that there were over ninety of us in that particular year. Living quarters were cramped as the bedrooms were really built for one person, but because of the size of our class, we were two to a room. Overall, I loved the eleven months of novitiate. I did not mind the discipline. Having spent time at Kings Point, the novitiate was easier. The whole period of time was focused on spirituality and trying to deepen one's understanding of what is entailed in the priesthood. We had wonderful times preparing and putting on our own entertainment shows, which were called "Gaudeamus," Latin for "let us rejoice." We were all obliged to have different responsibilities and each assignment was rotated every three months or so. One of those three month assignments was to be a social director. This forced me into seeking other classmates to volunteer for the shows. This also entailed visiting with the rector to ask permission on behalf of my classmates. I found it easy to approach the rector at that time and found he had a great sense of humor and a low-key style.*

*When we began our novitiate period, I had given up alcohol use, not because I realized that I had a problem with my use, but rather did so because I was entering the seminary. I did not drink during the two years we were studying philosophy. As we neared the close of our novitiate, a nearby family followed their custom of inviting the outgoing class to their house for an outdoor picnic. On that occasion I saw a lot of beer available and said to myself, "I'll just have one." It turned out that one led to another and then another and I got half crocked. To that point I had not taken a drink in almost three years. The next morning I asked myself what had happened that I drank having promised God I would not drink in thanksgiving for my vocation? In no way did I realize at that juncture that I was already into the early stages of the disease of alcoholism. I renewed my promise to God and did not drink again until January 1956 in Tanganyika. But the disease process had clearly begun.*

Jim never believed that he had a great mind for formal theological study. He did well in his studies, but a major effort was required on his part. Jim also was ready, willing, and anxious to be ordained and sent overseas. So the conclusion of theological studies came as a great relief. Maryknoll was bursting with new candidates for the order, but Jim had no desire to do further study or teach in one of the schools. He had been preparing for a specific mission and role. He was ready to ship out. Jim was ordained a priest on June 11, 1955, and assigned with many of his classmates to an area of Tanganyika that would later become the diocese of Shinyanga. As he prepared to board a ship for a journey from which he would not return for at least a decade, Jim said goodbye to his family and friends. Africa was a world away from the large house on Long Island. Because the assignment posed many physical hardships, his future was as uncertain as it had been when he joined the merchant marines. He could die in an accident or from a disease. His parents were getting older, his siblings having children and finding their own way in life. He was strengthened by the conviction that he was doing what God wanted him do to. Even so, he felt the sorrow of the departure and knew that once he boarded the ship, nothing in his life would ever be the same again. And then, like his great grandparents before him, Jim began the passage to a new and different life. In the process, Jim's promise to never drink again was broken, and he learned again that growing up required him to embrace the pain not just once, but every day of his life.

## FIVE

# *Summer Passages*

WITH EACH VISIT to Jim's room, it was clear to me that his illness was progressing. He stopped more often to take a breath, and his cheek bones were becoming more predominant. When I asked him how he felt, Jim replied, "About the way that I should." That was my signal not to ask for specific details. Observing that he thought I looked a little pale, he asked me what was happening in my illness. "You look beat," he said, "so it must be something." Reluctantly I told him that I was having recurrent kidney infections. I was taking powerful medicine to suppress my immune system as a way to control the arthritis. The combination of medications was working very well for the arthritis itself, but it appeared that my immune system was suppressed too much. I had been on antibiotics for a several weeks to control the infection. The day before I met with Jim, I had undergone tests to determine whether or not there was underlying kidney damage. My doctor didn't think so, but given that kidney problems are a known side effect of medications I had been taking for some time, we needed to be cautious and explore all possibilities. The disappointing part of the side effects was that I would likely need to stop taking the medication that had treated pain, but caused other problems. It would be a long journey to get the medication straightened out again.

Jim listened carefully to my story. "How's your spirit?" he asked.

"About the way it should be, I guess."

"Well," he said, "I'll pray for you. Be patient. And for crying out loud, turn this whole thing over to God. Otherwise it's going to drive you crazy." Then, ever the host, Jim motioned toward his nightstand and offered me a granola bar or, if I preferred, a can of Ensure.

I took the granola bar.

"Ensure tastes marginally better when it's cold, you know," I told Jim.

"I will try to remember that when the time comes for me to drink the stuff," Jim replied.

Jim was trying to hold off on the Ensure, as if drinking it were a concession to his illness. Like anyone, Jim revisited his acceptance and surrender of will daily, often in something as small as a can of chocolate supplement that makes up for lost calories. It is almost impossible to surrender everything simultaneously, and he was tending to one thing at a time.

Jim was making arrangements to work with the Phelps Hospital hospice team in the weeks ahead. Hospice specializes in palliative care and an improved quality of life for terminally ill patients and their families. Hospice would assist Jim in consciously addressing the final stage of life with attention to the emotional and spiritual preparation for death. The philosophy of hospice was consistent with Jim's own desires to die with dignity and at peace. The team would work with Jim and the nurses at St. Teresa's to manage his pain and assist him in his final weeks. He did not quite need the hospice team yet, but he knew that within a short time, he would be restricted to bed. "I am also holding off on going to bed until I absolutely have to," he said. "I like seeing people from this angle." Like the Ensure, going to bed was a concession that Jim did not yet have to make.

In the meantime, Jim was taking care of business. He had signed his car over to the Maryknoll Society since he saw no use in pretending that he would ever drive again. Jim was grateful that he didn't have to do all of the work of dying on the same day. With each thing that he let go of and each detail he tended, Jim was saying out loud that he accepted the reality of his impending death. He was also practicing his belief that everyone should take responsibility for themselves in all aspects of their lives. There was no need to leave a lot of work behind for someone else when Jim could still do it for himself.

That he could be so direct in handling his death gave me courage and patience. It also made me feel like a bit of a wimp since I was worrying about tests that would likely be fine while Jim handled the unenviable task of preparing for management of his pain from cancer. When I mentioned this to Jim, he reminded me that comparing oneself to others is always a good way to get into trouble, particularly if one is given to guilt. "There's always someone better or worse than you," he said often. "Be sensitive to others, learn from them, but pay honest attention to your own needs. Just don't waste a lot of time feeling sorry for yourself. Pay attention and then pray." Jim again suggested that I embrace my own pain, be compassionate to his, and let God take care of both of us. It was very good advice, and without having gone crazy, the next day I learned that my kidneys were just fine.

Jim could see that his time was growing shorter. He wanted to talk with me about Africa — the place where he had spent most of his life. Jim's face changed when he talked about Africa. It was as though his affection for the place and its people temporarily softened the signature of pain on his features. For Jim, remembering Africa was more than revisiting his youth; it was touching deeply at the heart of his spirit. I commented to Jim about the change that came over him. He was silent for a moment and then said, "Oh sure, I love to remember Africa. That is where my vocation and my recovery became real for me." The quality of his presence when he described his life in Africa became nothing less than a man saying goodbye to one of the great joys of his life.

When Jim was ordained in 1955, Maryknoll itself was only forty-four years old. The first generations of missioners were still alive. Maryknoll was originally founded for the missions in China, but World War II and the Chinese revolution had made it important for Maryknoll to expand its areas of operation. The first missioners to go to Africa and Latin America did so in 1945. Jim was going to a place that was a new territory — at least for Maryknoll. The work was in its early stages. One of the leaders in Maryknoll's efforts in Africa was Bishop Edward McGurkin. A gentle, committed, and generous man, the bishop sent fifteen men from the class of '55 to a huge area of what is now Tanzania. Their work would eventually expand the diocese of Shinyanga and provide a pastoral presence in some of the most isolated areas of the diocese. It was not work for the faint of heart, and luckily no one who left for Africa in 1955 fit that description. Least of all, Jim Lenihan.

Tanzania is in East Africa, bordered by the Indian Ocean and located between Kenya to the north and Mozambique to the south. It is slightly larger than twice the size of California, but less than 4 percent of the land is arable. Yet 90 percent of the 35 million people who live there engage in agriculture. The land is plagued by crop failures and drought followed by flooding, yet most commerce and industry in the country is related to agriculture. Tanzania is one of the poorest countries in the world with life expectancy listed as fifty-two, which takes into account a high infant mortality rate. The population is young, and at this moment in history, suffering a pandemic of AIDS. Mount Kilimanjaro, at 19,341 feet the highest peak in Africa, is in Tanzania. The Great Rift Valley, a magnificent geological fault system that extends from the Middle East to Mozambique, passes through Tanzania. The coastline is a thousand miles long with the islands of Zanzibar and Pemba being part of the Republic of Tanzania.

The beauty and diversity of the country is breathtaking as are the poverty and complexity of peoples, cultures, and languages. There are more than 120 different tribes and local languages, a history of colonization and tribal self-sufficiency, and only one medical doctor for every twenty-five thousand people. It is a far cry from life in the United States or from the common misperceptions of Africa.

"What did you think when you first arrived in Africa?" I asked Jim.

Leaning back in his chair, he replied by asking me "What did you think when you first arrived in Latin America?"

"I thought that it was the most incredible place that I had ever seen. And I thought that I was in way over my head and that I would never learn the language."

"Arriving in Africa was something like that," Jim replied. "Only it took a lot longer to get there, which meant it would take a lot longer to get home. I was sure God wanted me to be there, and that gave me confidence beyond what I would have had on my own. I had prayed for an assignment to Africa, and I was thrilled when I received one. Now learning the language, that was another story. There was Kiswahili to learn. That is the language of the Bantu. Official things are done in English. But if I wanted to be a pastor, I knew that I had to learn local languages. Our mission was simple in those days — we were bringing the Catholic Church to Africa. All I had to do was figure out how to do that."

Life in Africa demanded all of Jim Lenihan, including a willingness to change his sense of home. Everything was different from what he knew. The vast, rural area of the diocese was quite unlike Brooklyn. The customs of the people were hard to comprehend, the work was physically challenging, and there were no luxuries to soften the blow of being in a new place. Jim was newly ordained and facing the difficulties of learning how to be a pastor among a people whose language he could barely comprehend. And yet he was falling in love with Tanzania. The hospitality of the people and the wonder of the land spoke deeply to Jim. Adjusting to life in Africa required significant patience and willingness to let go. In retrospect, Jim believed that his already active alcoholism kept him from surrendering fully to God and the new experience. "It made me rush everything," he said. Nonetheless, Jim entered into his life and work in Africa with passion and commitment.

Jim, who had first gone to work as a butcher's delivery boy when he was seven years old, felt at home with the other hard-working Maryknoll missioners. The Maryknoll fathers, brothers, and sisters built schools, parishes, medical dispensaries, and cooperatives all over Tanzania. The missioners saw education as a pressing need, and all worked hard in that apostolate. At that time, building the church in Africa often literally meant getting involved with brick and mortar while tending to the daily pastoral needs of the people. Jim had straightforward dreams that gave him strength in his first years in Africa. Not believing himself to be a "genius for languages," Jim wanted to listen well and learn to speak the language of the Basukuma people who lived in the Shinyanga diocese. He also wanted to be able to relax with the Basukuma in their own language and in their own way. "If I could relax with them," he told me, "I would know that we trusted each other. I also knew that to reach that level of trust would take some time." The tribal language that Jim was trying to learn has been identified by linguists as comparable in difficulty to a native English speaker learning Russian. Jim nonetheless learned to listen well and to communicate with the Basukuma — if not perfectly, with a care that earned him respect and trust.

Initially working as a curate with the Missioners of Africa, Jim held on to his dreams and learned the day-to-day realities of being a "parish priest" in Africa. There were six parishes in the newly formed diocese of Shinyanga. The town of Shinyanga sat next to the railroad built by German colonists during their occupation of Tanganyika. When World War I and the tsetse fly drove the Germans back to Europe, the British colonized Tanganyika. The British took advantage of the limited infrastructure successfully completed and used the railroad to transport crops and other materials. However, they built a railroad with a different gauge track than the Germans, thus laying the foundation for transportation problems within the country.

The sound of the trains passing through Shinyanga gave the impression that the country — and the track — went on forever. The same impression was given to the naked eye. The land seemed as vast as the sea and required just as much patience and respect. Outstations of the parishes extended sixty miles in any direction. Jim traveled by motorcycle to meet the faithful who gathered for baptisms, marriages, celebration of Eucharist, and catechesis. He learned to be prepared to respond to the people who were waiting for him in the outstation and to listen to those who wanted to speak to the priest. Jim visited the sick, brought communion, and anointed the dying.

There was no end to the suffering or the hospitality that Jim encountered in the outstations. He shared many happy meals with catechists and leaders who opened their humble homes, offering what little they had and opening their hearts. Like the Lenihan Sunday dinners, the hospitality and shared meals of Shinyanga deepened the spirit of Eucharist for Jim. He was busy and got caught up in the energy of becoming familiar with the new culture.

In 1959, Jim moved to a new area of the Shinyanga diocese to oversee the building of a church, rectory, and small school. His living space was literally built over his head while he worked to make education possible in the villages. He learned to sit quietly and listen to the tribal chiefs and government officials as he sought to attend to the physical and spiritual needs of the people. Jim's patience paid off. He came to be trusted by the local leaders, who assisted him in building a school, a medical dispensary, and a two-year training program for catechists from the whole diocese. Within a few years, Jim moved on to build the church — literally and symbolically — in another area of the diocese. For a year he lived in a grass-roofed mud hut while the new church and rectory were built. This church was at the farthest end of the diocese and sixty miles from any other parish. Often Jim walked ten miles or more to see parishioners or walked home from a ride that only took him part way to the rectory. The black soil in the area grew great cotton, but in the rainy season it made entering or leaving the area impossible for months at a time.

"There is no describing how isolated that place is," says Maryknoll Brother Kevin Dargan. "Even in the dry season, it is very hard to get there. In the rainy season, Jim was on his own." Jim's alcoholism was by then in an active phase, as was his cigar smoking. The isolation of the rainy season caused a problem in the area that all addicts most closely monitor: supply of their substance of choice. For Jim, that required making sure that he had an adequate supply of beer and cigars to last through the rainy season. As he became more familiar with the area, Jim worked out a supply line that included the delivery of a storeroom full of beer by way of lorries. The cigars were made in a Ugandan cooperative that was run by another missionary order. Somehow the cigars found their way across the Tanzanian border and were distributed to customers by bicycle. The cigars were hand packed, wrapped in banana leaves, and of dubious quality. The unevenness of the packing caused the cigars to be known both to put themselves out and to suddenly spurt a larger flame — events that generally took the smoker by surprise. Despite the problems with the cigars, Jim claimed that smoking them kept the mosquitoes away. No one believed him because Jim appeared to be the only person for whom the pungent mosquito repellant was effective. Most people simply — and correctly — assumed that Jim was hooked on smoking cigars. It was unlikely that any of the people around him knew the story of his bad decision toward independence.

By all accounts, including his own, Jim's storeroom was something to behold in the last days of the dry season. The beer was stacked neatly along one side of the room, piles of cigars resting in their banana leaf wrappers on the other side. Jim was ready for the rain and blissfully unaware of how excessive his preparations seemed to those not caught in the grips of addiction. While unbelievably isolated at the end of the diocese, Jim spent the rainy season ministering to the people of the area. At the end of the day — whatever time that might be — he retired to his house and worked on depleting his storeroom supplies. At the end of the rainy season, the lorries returned to carry away the empty bottles. The bottles clinking together on rough roads made a loud and memorable noise. Trying to lessen the sound, Jim hoarded cardboard to put between the empty bottles, thus expanding his concern for rainy-day supplies into a year-long hobby, and obsession.

True to the dynamics of alcoholism, neither Jim nor anyone around him talked directly about the craziness of his behavior. It was simply perceived as the way Jim was. Jim wanted to keep his illness and struggles to himself. His physical surroundings proved to be only the outward expression of an internal isolation that made him fear abandonment if he burdened other people with his problems. That lonely dynamic is at the core of alcoholism. The irony is that the behavior of the active alcoholic can be much more of a burden than speaking the truth.

His active illness not withstanding, Jim grew in language proficiency and understanding of the culture. Young priests from Maryknoll and the local church were often assigned to work with him. The priests would stay with Jim for a few months and then be transferred to other assignments. He served as that type of guide for years. Those who served with him remember him as very hospitable and challenging. Jim told new people that the only way to get started was to jump in and get busy. New priests emulated his example. Jim had gained the trust of the local leaders, the church, and the people of his area — both Christian and non-Christian. He shared life with people who were "gentle and loving and the most hospitable people in the world."

Jim lived, worked, and prayed in a country that was going through the process of first becoming an independent nation and then trying to establish within itself a just social order. Forming an independent nation was a very difficult process because of the vast territory and the artificial boundaries that had been drawn by Europeans. Independence was won for Tanganyika in 1961 under the leadership of Julius Nyerere. Educated in Maryknoll schools, Nyerere was a man of peace with a vision of independence based on interdependence and rejection of the lingering attitudes and effects of colonialism. The new nation of Tanzania came into being in 1964 when Tanganyika joined with the islands of Zanzibar and Pemba. The joy of independence, nationalization of the economy, and attempts to build on the extended family — *ujamaa* — created great hope in the country.

The sense of newness and hope in the nation were mirrored by the energy and excitement in the church that was created by the Second Vatican Council. "Change in the church often begins in the missions," says Father Tom McDonnell, a Maryknoll priest who served first as a curate to Jim Lenihan in 1965 and later as the administrator of St. Teresa's Residence where Jim died. "The council caught up with some of those changes, such as mass in the vernacular and empowerment of the laity. When we were ordained and sent to Africa, the veteran missioners were anxious to talk to us about our studies of the Vatican documents in the seminary. The combination of the declaration of African interdependence and the Vatican Council created an unbelievable level of energy and hope. Jim was part of that energy. As newly ordained priests, we lionized him. He was our hero."

The hero knew all too well that he stood on clay feet and eventually asked to be relieved of his responsibilities as a mentor. Part of the reason that he tired of the role was that he couldn't stand the emptiness when the young priests went on to other assignments and he had to adjust to being alone again. Exciting as the times were, and as much as he enjoyed working with young priests, it simply felt easier to live alone.

What Jim did not write into his outlines or tell me in our conversations was how much his mentoring meant to new missioners. When Bill Murphy was first sent to Tanzania in 1971, he was assigned to work with Jim. Bill recalls, "I was fresh out of language school when I went to Nyalikungu to work with Jim. He was really my first and most formative introduction to the African people. Jim loved the Sukuma people. He knew, understood, and loved their culture. He knew them both as individuals and as a group. He did not just work with them; he spent most of his leisure time with Africans in their homes. And Jim did not limit his friendship or concern to Christians only. He had many Moslem friends, and numerous people of native religions sought him out, both as a friend and as a missioner. Jim had an excellent command of the Sukuma language and could joke with people in their own dialect. He also enjoyed Sukuma traditional music. I was a young and impressionable missioner, and Jim made a very deep impression on me. I'll always be grateful to have first met the African people through the loving, compassionate, and mirthful eyes of Jim Lenihan."

Jim also failed to mention — though I believe he knew — that twenty years after he left Tanzania, people in the areas where he worked still remember and talk about him. They remember his kindness, his gentleness, and his persistence. That Jim did not mention the regard in which he was held was consistent with his insistence that whatever good he did in life was a result of God working through him. I called Jim's attention to a letter of thanks that he had given

74

me in the papers. It was written by Bishop McGurkin when he returned to the United States in 1975:

Dear Jim,

This is just a short note to say goodbye as I get ready to leave Shinyanga and start for the States. Also, I want to thank you for all your very wonderful cooperation through the years, for having made my own job so easy in many ways and in so many areas.

Right from the start, back in 1955, it was truly great the way that you got into things with your co-workers. [Your parish]...covered such a large area. You certainly had the major part in making a start in getting this going. And I know that besides putting all your work and energy into these missions, you also put a lot of your own money into setting up the places and keeping them going.... Besides all of this pastoral work, you have always cooperated generously and intelligently in diocesan efforts. It should be very rewarding for you to look back at these places and know that so much of what you accomplished with a lot of sweat and trouble and expense is carrying on and continuing in some measure what you hoped it would do. And so, I feel that I have good reason to say: Many, many thanks, Jim. You have been and are a truly

great missioner. Thanks again for everything.
God bless you. Please keep me in your prayers.

Sincerely in our Lord,
Edward McGurkin

"That was a nice letter," Jim said with a sly smile.
"Bishop McGurkin was a great man."

For the moment, I gave up the fight to help Jim
appreciate himself. It was not until very near the end
of his life that he could truly receive how much he
was loved for himself. That proved to be his final
lesson in humility and acceptance.

The hope for social changes in Tanzania was
soon eclipsed by a lack of international cooperation, a dearth of petroleum resources, and failure
of African partnerships. Tanzania was economically
and politically isolated in many ways. While some of
Tanzania's neighbors endured horrific dictatorships,
Tanzania clung to its social vision. The remnants
of colonialism, however, were reshaped in the Cold
War. Western nations rejected the peaceful vision
of Nyerere as too socialistic and offered little assistance to a country trying to find a new way. Nyerere
stood firm in his position that Tanzania was neither
communist nor capitalist but explicitly African. The
uniqueness of the Tanzanian vision found few lis-
teners in the world. The changes of Vatican II were

sweeping yet unevenly embraced. That created conflict not only within the church but in the analysis of what mission to the modern world really means.

As always, international decisions, national movements, and devastating tragedies played out in the lives of individuals and families in Tanzania. All questioning and change aside, the need for pastoral care and physical assistance became all the more pressing in the 1960s and 1970s. The 1980s saw the beginnings of the AIDS pandemic. Rainfall amounts in Tanzania have always been unpredictable in Shinyanga, and the alternating drought and flooding were disastrous. No matter what the situation, local leaders, families, Jim, and other missioners worked to the point of exhaustion trying to meet the needs of the people. Jim anointed the sick, buried the dead, witnessed innocent human beings suffering. And he celebrated with the people — births, weddings, festivals. Jim learned that harmony in relationships is a generative value in Africa, one that matched his own family experience.

As a way of communicating to the Lenihans about his life in Africa, Jim made a home movie in about 1970. The film begins as the ship travels down the East River toward open seas. The next shot is the contrasting skyline of Dar es Salaam. The film documents the pastoral work in Shinyanga. Watching the shaky, silent images of the film, I was impressed by the sheer numbers of people ministered to by Jim. A third of the film shows the digging of a well, hard physical labor in which Jim and other missioners assisted. The film of that project leaves no doubt that water is the basis for life. The film brings into one silent sequence the journey, the sacraments, and the thirst for living water that defined Jim's service in Africa — a statement about how Jim understood his life there.

Though living in Tanzania was a challenge to stamina and faith, at the time Jim considered himself to be very happy. Like many missioners that I have known, Jim spoke of his experience in Africa as though it were really all quite ordinary — and for Jim it was. I reminded Jim that not everyone lived through wars of independence or spent their vacations on safari in a stunning land. While Jim admitted that was true, he said that he spent most of his days engaged in very ordinary activity: the water projects, fixing his motorcycle, or repairing a hole in the roof. The sacraments were celebrated in the daily round and the larger cycle of life in Africa.

Jim sternly warned me against making him into "some kind of hero" in my mind or in the retelling of his story. What mattered most to Jim was not that he had experienced extraordinary things in Africa or at other moments in his life. What mattered to him was that he tried to live faithfully to his primary vocation — to be a loving human being. It was from that love that his priestly vocation was born. "I've loved my life as a missionary priest," he said. "It has been a good expression for my own talents, gifts, and interests. I did what I thought God made me to do and it gave me joy. Everybody is called to do the same thing — I just happened to be called to do it in a different land." I agreed with Jim that we are all called to dedicate our lives to service, give expression to our deepest gifts, and hand our lives over to God.

Yet I also knew that to follow through on the sacrifice needed to be so fully alive in one's soul requires a kind of quiet heroism that is unusual. I had a difficult time finding that kind of courage in my own heart. Jim's witness reminded me that one of the most difficult sacrifices to make is letting go of the illusion that we are in control of our lives. We must hand ourselves over to God in the smallest of things. In reality, that requires remarkably deep surrender. For Jim that surrender happened only after the extraordinary missioner came to accept the reality that he was, in the parlance of AA, an ordinary drunk.

As the story of his rainy season storeroom demonstrates, the promise Jim made after the picnic in 1955 to never drink again had long since dissolved. In retrospect, Jim believed that he was entering into the middle stages of his illness during the years when he was mentoring new priests and working very hard as a missioner. Looking back on those years from the perspective of sobriety, Jim wrote:

*I would characterize that period in my life as using people and God as objects, a lot of selfish and sick behavior. It was all Jim's way. I did not understand the paradox of giving and receiving. I thought that all of the love and work came from me. I was totally in control. I couldn't receive from others. Jesus allowed himself to receive visitors; he accepted lodging and meals from others; he sought and arranged for periodic times to leave people and go to a quiet place to receive strength in prayer. He allowed a young man to give of his few loaves and fishes, which turned into the miracle of feeding thousands of people. He accepted the hospitality of an unnamed person who supplied the house and preparations for the last meal with his friends before his death. I could not allow myself to receive in that way. In receiving, there is no control; in giving, we do have some control. I did not have the humility to receive graciously from the African people. I thought that I had all of the answers and that if people just did what I said, they would be fine. I am not saying that God did not work through me in those years. It is simply that I now know that my attitudes were selfish and reflected the progression of my chronic illness. I wasn't honest with myself about my drinking, so I could not be honest in relationships. I was manipulative and out of touch with myself. Everyone became an object for me — something for me to "fix."*

*In those years we had many social gatherings. The attendance was always high and often we would stay overnight or sometimes two nights. These were great times for us. It was during such occasions that we often exchanged experiences in our work and listened to others. The spirit in the diocese was very good. In addition, there was a lot of heavy drinking at these affairs. Just from an alcoholic point of view, it was "paradise." All in the open and drinking with others. Not everyone drank or drank to excess, but I would be among those who would continue on for hours. Looking back to this period from today's sobriety, I realize that I was a functional alcoholic and at the same time sloppy. I rushed things needlessly and lost control of my alcohol use. My relationships were affected by my alcohol use, and I was very dishonest with myself as my life came to revolve around alcohol use.*

The people around Jim were aware of his alcohol use. A friend of Jim's remembers that during the 1960s after several beers, and often in the midst of a party he had thrown, Jim would quietly mention to someone the fear that his drinking was out of control. Yet for all of his internal suffering, people remember Jim as "the happiest drunk in town." While drinking he was friendly and hospitable, holding parties and procuring special food treats through a series of connections he had made with local merchants. He was functional and did excellent pastoral work.

It was a great strain to be the happiest drunk when Jim felt internal emptiness and shame. As is so often the case, Jim's secret was public knowledge. Yet whether drinking or not, everyone thought of Jim as a pleasant, open, and hospitable person. Every year Jim "proved" that his drinking was under control by giving up alcohol for Lent. He was aware of the joke among his peers that he stashed alcohol in the church so that it would be readily available on Easter Sunday. He later declared that he would never have been involved in that type of sacrilege. He did admit, however, to keeping the alcohol in a place where he could reach it moments after mass ended on Easter Sunday. At the time, it did not strike him as problematic that he started drinking again as soon as Lent ended. In his mind, the annual ritual proved to Jim that he could "stop anytime." He had everything — and everybody — under control.

Like many alcoholics, Jim was the last one to know the truth about what controlled his life, and to make that discovery he had to travel home geographically not once, but twice. The journey to finally be at home with himself required some intervention and a great deal of care.

# SIX

# Homecomings

O NE OF JIM'S goals as a missioner was to develop Christian communities that were self-sufficient and not dependent upon him. By 1976, he believed that he had been successful in that goal. In the area where he was working there was a Tanzanian priest prepared to take over the sacramental responsibilities for him. The communities were strong, and Jim was called back to the United States to begin a three-year assignment in fundraising and mission education based in Long Island. As Jim was making the trip home, his friend and first superior Bishop Edward McGurkin wrote to the superior general of Maryknoll saying, "We are sending you our best — Jim Lenihan."

Returning to the United States was bittersweet for Jim. Life had changed in the two decades that he had been gone; nieces and nephews were born and raised without having Uncle Jim as part of their daily lives. Jim deeply loved his siblings and their children, and he grieved for what he had missed in their lives. Both of Jim's parents and his sister Betty were

dead. Within a year of his arrival in New York, Jim
would bury his brother Paul. There was a tremen-
dous sense of loss not only because of the deaths but
also because of a fundamental sense of having been
uprooted — first when he left New York and then
when returning from a once foreign land that Jim
had come to deeply love. "I was given a lot of preparation to go to Africa," Jim observed. "I didn't have
any preparation to return home. Nor did I know how
difficult it would be."

Jim's job required that he visit parishes and schools
telling his mission story and inviting others to become a part of Maryknoll — either as a donor or
as an expression of their own religious vocation. Jim
lived and worked with another Maryknoll priest who
was a good friend. Jim's drinking and restlessness
were by then a secret only to him. Recognizing that
all was not right with Jim, his religious superiors
suggested that he seek counseling. Jim met with a
psychologist for several sessions. Jim found the sessions pleasant and he liked the counselor, but he did
not feel that he was receiving much from the process.
When Jim raised these doubts to the psychologist, he
told Jim that he did not see any reason for their work
to continue because, said Jim, he "could find nothing
wrong with me. He said he would send a report to
Maryknoll saying the same thing. I never heard any
more about counseling — at least then. Looking back

I realize that he never once asked me about my drinking, and since I was at that point an active alcoholic, I certainly didn't bring the subject up."

Jim had done what was asked of him, was declared well, and continued to drink daily. The people concerned about Jim were happy that he had followed through on the recommendation for help. Jim had been unhappy for so long that he recognized that state as normal. He marked the sessions with the psychologist as meaningless and put them away in his mind. There was no need to go into anything any further. Jim would later instruct others never to expect active alcoholics to volunteer information — or tell the truth — about their drinking. "Nobody is going to tell you the truth about something they think they need to stay alive and that they are afraid you'll take away from them," he said. Jim's denial kept his alcoholism active and his restlessness undiagnosed.

Denial is a defense mechanism that most of us know quite a bit about. It can protect us from information that is overwhelming and at times make it possible to survive the unspeakable. In some life circumstances, denial is required to get through the day. A certain level of it exists in all of us at any given moment. Yet when used consistently as a way to avoid the realities of life, denial can slip into a pathology that alienates a human being from themselves and from God. Denial then becomes a process of moving around limited pieces of understanding in the hope that they will create a different picture. Denial can easily fall into what AA literature describes as "the craziness of trying the same thing over and over again with the expectation of a different result."

I learned more about denial than I wanted to know through my experience with depression and with rheumatoid arthritis. Years into successful treatment for depression and experienced enough to know better, I suggested to my psychiatrist that perhaps I didn't need to take medication any longer. After all, I argued, I do not feel depressed. The doctor gently pointed out that the reason I no longer felt depressed most likely was directly linked to the medication, and since we know there is such a strong biological component to the illness, perhaps I should not be so anxious to abandon medication. It was a bit of a blow to my ego to realize that I had fallen into a familiar trap for people who must depend on medication: declare yourself well and stop taking medicine the minute that it finally works.

Realizing that the doctor was right, I seemed to have to start all over again in accepting that depression is part of my life and, treated or not, likely will be as long as I live. Yet the unnamed demon is always harder to live with and befriend. Once I got over the initial blow to my pride, there was relief in accepting yet again that I have a disease — or two. I felt very vulnerable and at the same time empowered.

I had a similar experience with rheumatoid arthritis. Because the disease can sometimes be so draining, it is common for people who have it to think, "I must have something other than 'just arthritis.'" Preferably, I must have something that is easily cured. After my initial diagnosis, I saw two different rheumatologists who agreed that I had the disease and recommended the same course of treatment. I was compliant with the treatment, but deep down, I knew that it was all a mistake. I was imagining my symptoms. I had Lyme disease. Maybe I really was just allergic to nightshade vegetables. Then I answered an ad looking for research subjects at the Hospital for Joint Diseases in Manhattan. I went to the hospital for an examination, interview, x-rays, and extensive blood work. By then I had been on aggressive treatment for three years, and I still thought that it was all a mistake. I fully expected to be thrown out of the research clinic as an "imposter," hopefully with a ten-day supply of something that would make it all go away.

It was not enough to me that the rheumatologist who examined me found more than enough swollen and tender joints to confirm the diagnosis on the spot. I finally believed that I had the disease two weeks later when I received a call from the nurse at the research clinic. I met the criteria for the genetic study because I carried the marker gene for susceptibility to rheumatoid arthritis. An amazing calm settled over me when I received that call. All of the pain, all of the difficulty was not of my doing. I really, truly had a disease. I was suffering not because I was weak or had eaten too many Twinkies as a child. When I called a friend to tell her that I had matched the genetic criteria for the study, she told me, "I have never heard anyone so happy about carrying the gene for a disease."

My happiness was not that I had the gene or the disease(s). I felt relief that denial, which had for a time felt life-saving, fell away from my heart. I wish I could say that at that moment the denial left me once and for all, but that was not the case. To truly overcome denial, we must not only accept the diagnosis but also embrace vulnerability and let God be God. That process takes a lifetime because it strikes at the heart of human pride, arrogance, and a sense of invincibility. Denial stakes a claim in the human soul by making false promises that vulnerability will never be experienced, diseases are for other people, and perfection is possible. When the hollowness of those promises is exposed, the result is often a crisis and a change of heart is possible. Or, if the denial rebounds, we may run from the truth as if our lives

depended on it, which many times in a twisted form
of understanding, it does.

Denial is at the heart of alcoholism. Those who
recognize the effects of alcohol on their lives and immediately address them are on the road to recovery of
their sanity. For many alcoholics, as for many others
using denial as a chief way of being in the world, it
takes more than one pass at the truth before the heart
comprehends reality. So it was for Jim. After meeting with the counselor and being "declared well,"
Jim continued to be in the grip of denial of his alcoholism. "I knew what was best for myself and for
everyone else," Jim said. "I knew that I didn't have
a drinking problem because I could still function."
For the alcoholic, denial can persist in the face of
overwhelming evidence like loss of job and family, a
conviction for driving under the influence, blackouts,
and physical injury. More than refusing to acknowledge the impact of alcohol in one's life, denial in this
context is nothing less than casting oneself in the role
of God. Only the alcoholic knows what is best for his
or her life.

Jim continued to function, continued his work,
and continued to drink. After two and a half years
of a three-year assignment, Jim asked to return immediately to Tanzania. Jim's superiors asked him to
give a reason for what he later described as a "sick
request," but he could not give them one. Jim simply

knew that he was restless and tired. He blamed those feelings on the work that he was doing, and he was absolutely certain that he would feel better as soon as he returned to Africa. Jim's friends and colleagues were still concerned about him, but because of the respect that people had for him, Jim's request was honored. Jim was given permission to return to Africa.

Jim did not know then that he was making what the addiction literature refers as "a geographic escape." A symptom of alcoholism, the escape is motivated by the false belief that a "change of scenery" will solve all of the alcoholic's problems. Blaming all difficulty on a particular environment, the alcoholic will try to change everything all at once. Geographic escapes fall under an umbrella that many of us hold overhead when unacceptable reality threatens to intrude. We resort to the comfort of "if only." If only I could work with different people. If only I were better understood. If only I could change someone else. If only life did not have so much pain. If only I could return to Africa.

Jim was uniquely able to exercise the option of a geographic escape because of his missionary priesthood. With relative ease, he went ten thousand miles away from the problems he was experiencing on Long Island. What he could not claim in that moment was that he had brought his alcoholism with him, and as a result within a few weeks he experienced the disappointment of discovering that within him nothing had changed. If anything, the relocation caused new questions and doubts and eventually made him feel guilty that he had used his missionary priesthood in service of his denial.

Jim returned to an externally complicated situation. There had been changes in pastoral approach and policy on the diocesan level that were painful for Jim. He found that he lacked trust in some important relationships and was dishonest with his peers and with himself. Jim's previous work was completed, and he needed to search for a new understanding of himself as a missioner. He drank for comfort, for companionship, and for courage. Jim was elected by his peers to a position of regional leadership. Their respect and trust contrasted with his own feelings of inadequacy and guilt. The alcohol was taking a toll on him emotionally, physically, and spiritually, registered in part by the fact that Jim had absolutely no recognition of the problem. And he was most certainly not volunteering information about his drinking to anyone else.

The next "if only" option for Jim was the belief that if he understood more about what was happening in mission around the world, he would be happy. Hoping for an "intellectual cure," in 1980 Jim registered for a renewal program back in New York.

He knew that he was very tired, and the idea of renewal appealed to him. As he was leaving Africa, it was suggested to Jim that he consult the staff of the Maryknoll Fathers and Brothers personnel office before he returned. Jim agreed, not foreseeing the topic of the meeting. When Jim went to the personnel office, he learned that his friends had been quite specific about drinking being the issue of concern. Jim was surprised at the suggestion that he have an evaluation for alcoholism, but he did not resist the idea. He had run out of "if only" options, and he didn't know what else to do. Jim went for a four-day evaluation and was diagnosed as suffering from the disease of alcoholism.

When Jim received the diagnosis, he responded much as I did when I learned that I carried the gene for rheumatoid arthritis. He felt a sense of relief. "I didn't have to hide anymore," he told me. "By 1980 I was afraid of people, and I needed to face myself and God and reverse that fear. The truth was out. When you've been killing yourself and trying to keep denial going, you lose energy. I was relieved to know that there was something that could be done."

The diagnosis of alcoholism — like the subsequent diagnosis of cancer — presented Jim with a fundamental question about how he wanted to live the rest of his life. Jim's acceptance and decision to be vital in the face of terminal cancer was, by his telling, an easy path. With the diagnosis of alcoholism, Jim had begun to embrace his own humanity, limitations, and imperfections. That embrace set the pattern for his life. When the cancer came, he knew what to do with the diagnosis. He did what he had been doing since 1980. He admitted his humanity, took a deep breath, and moved into the experience with as much courage as he could muster and God could give him.

*Through the intervention of other Maryknollers who cared about me, in 1980 I realized that I had become an alcoholic. When I was able to identify with the chronic disease of alcoholism — and the fact that it was treatable — I joined a recovery program. I look upon my alcoholism as a great blessing in my life. Though I looked upon alcohol as a friend, I realize that what it did was prolong my childhood. Thus, in recovery, I had to make many attitudinal changes in my life along with growing up emotionally. Recovery helps me to try to face realities in life. To appreciate I have limitations as a human being and also limited responsibilities. This has brought me an inner peace and freedom in my life today. It is for some of these factors that I can say I am glad I am an alcoholic. Otherwise I would never have started to grow up.*

Immediately after his diagnosis, Jim began to attend meetings of Alcoholics Anonymous. Following the recommendation of his sponsor, Jim attended ninety meetings in ninety days. There he began to unravel the impact and meaning of his disease and discovered the freedom that came from saying out loud, "My name is Jim and I am an alcoholic." The isolation of denial gave way to connection and hope.

*AA taught me that I could be part of a larger human community. That sense of connection melted away an old feeling of isolation and, curiously, made me feel less alone. It was not simply the alcoholism that frightened me; it was the terrible prospect of recognizing my own vulnerability and mortality. I did not want to accept responsibility for whether or not I am happy, or allow for the possibility that my happiness might depend on my not trying to run my own life without outside help or facing the reality that I do need other people and God. AA made those lessons clear.*

His gratitude for alcoholism was sincere. Jim really did consider it one of the great gifts of his life. Without it, he claimed, he would never have met the living God. Recovery from alcoholism requires nothing less than a total change of heart and in that conversion, faith has flesh and bones. AA promises that embracing the Twelve Step program and its foundation of rigorous honesty will bring about a total change in outlook toward life. Maintaining that change requires daily dedication.

Ninety meetings in ninety days were thus only the beginning for Jim. He had found in the recovery process and in the people he met at AA a pattern for living that spoke to the deepest needs of his heart. Jim formed friendships in AA that would last for the rest of his life. Within those relationships and Jim's growing sense of freedom, he experienced a sense of home he had been longing for since his days in the merchant marines. After so many years of isolation, denial, and fear, he had come home to himself. Jim diligently did the work of recovery. Each day he meditated on AA literature, worked the steps, talked with his sponsor, attended meetings. And each day he rediscovered that his life had just started again.

Even as the cancer spread and his movement became more restricted, Jim was still able to attend AA meetings. Someone from his home group picked him up and took him to the meetings. His sponsor regularly visited him, as did other members of the group. Jim's eighteenth anniversary of sobriety was to be celebrated at the end of the summer. He really wanted to attend that anniversary meeting and set it as a goal for himself. The AA daily readings were always at his bedside and he drew strength from them. "After eighteen years," he said "it would be a shame to lose my sobriety now." There was little chance of that. The readings and the contact with his AA group kept Jim's attitude and spirit consistent with what he had come to believe at the beginning of his recovery. To stay sane in the moment, he needed a power greater than himself.

Jim wrestled with the issue of taking medication for his pain. He had lived almost two decades substance free. He felt strange taking strong pain relievers. He hated feeling drowsy from the medication — it was too much like being drunk. By his own admission, he did not want to lose control. Through work with his sponsor and the hospice team, Jim came to understand that the medications were absolutely necessary and not a slip in his sobriety. He never really became comfortable with the medications, however. As he began to need stronger medicine more often to keep the pain under control, he demanded that he be allowed to manage his own medicine. The hospice nurses helped him to understand the medications and when to take them.

He kept careful track of what he took and when. He began to show me his medication records whenever I visited. Jim wrote his notes on pieces of green scrap paper: the name of the drug, the amount taken, and the time of day. He asked me if I knew about the various medications. The only one that I really knew

about was prednisone, a steroid that I was also taking to control my arthritis. When I told that to Jim
he said, "No kidding," and smiled, adding, "Some of
these drugs are good for whatever ails you." Then he
asked me about my experience of side effects. I tried
to tell him that I was on a much lower dose than he
was, that drug reactions are idiosyncratic, and that I
don't practice medicine without a license. He would
hear none of it. Promising not to sue, Jim coaxed the
side effects out of me. When I told him that the side
effects I experienced were nervousness and sleep dis-
turbance, he said, "That sounds like fun." I wasn't
sure if he said that for my benefit or for his. In either
case, he had just reminded me not to be afraid to
tell others the troubles that are sometimes a cause of
great fear. Jim was not running away from his reality,
and thanks to his example, neither was I. We decided
to be nervous together.

Jim admitted, however, that his approach to the
medication was a control issue on his part. He also
knew that his control over the medication process
would not last long. Jim confessed to me, "I think
that I'm driving the staff crazy about the medicine,
but I just have to know what I am taking, when, and
why." The need for such knowledge was one of the
few places that Jim stubbornly held on to his own
will. For whatever reason, that holding on gave him
dignity. He knew that when the time came, he would

let go of that last piece of control as well. And he was right that his insistence was driving people crazy. Jim didn't think that it was the first time he had had that effect on someone. He just didn't see any reason to rush the inevitable, and everyone who tried to argue the point with Jim — myself among them — rather quickly conceded defeat. As Jim was wont to say, no one is perfect. Truthfully, I was rather relieved at his control need. I was tempted to make him super-human, no matter how many times he warned me that making other people into heroes and deities is a good way to miss God's real point. We are loved as we are, and that is enough.

Jim certainly did not feel that he had achieved perfection or total freedom after his initial months of participation in AA. Having regained his physi-cal health, he experienced an unprecedented sense of peace. He began to feel that the alcoholism was be-hind him. Jim had admitted to himself that he was an alcoholic, recovery gave him joy, and he no longer had any desire to drink. While on retreat, Jim spoke with his spiritual director about his deep feelings of serenity. The spiritual director was also in recovery from alcoholism. He advised Jim to "pray for anxi-ety." Jim recalled laughing out loud at this advice. It seemed that recovery was freeing him from anxiety. Why would he want to experience it again?

*He then gently explained that we should not seek
needless anxiety but some anxiety is normal in all
of our lives in order to challenge us to grow. I have
been a slow pupil in how to live, and this was new
information for me. I didn't want growth if anxiety
was part of the package! Yet learning this truth was
a blessing for me. That piece of spiritual direction
challenges me every day of my life and has helped me
greatly in dealing with avoiding needless anxiety. It
has also taught me not to be afraid of growing pains.*

Alcohol had kept Jim from truly experiencing
many of the normal human emotions. Growing in
sobriety requires becoming more emotionally aware,
to feel what is happening within, and to act on those
feelings in healthy ways.

Feeling appropriate anxiety, as well as excitement
and anticipation, Jim returned to Africa in 1981 to
continue his recovery. If Africa had provided a geo
graphic escape for Jim during his illness, returning
to Africa would offer an opportunity to grow in
sobriety. Living in the place where his illness had pro
gressed was important to Jim's recovery. He needed
to make amends to people he had hurt, and he
wanted to work in a very different way. After working for years as a pastor in Tanzania, Jim requested
that he be assigned as a curate. He asked for this assignment so that he would not immediately become

overly involved and begin working in his familiar
style. Jim knew that his sobriety could be lost at any
time. He returned to people he knew and trusted, and
some that he did not. Jim brought a new set of tools
with him to Africa in the form of his daily recovery
meditations and activities.

*When I returned to an area where many people
knew me, some would approach me and say that they
had noticed I was not drinking. I replied that I realized that drinking had become a problem in my life.
Some would ask me what* lbugota *(medicine) I was
using to stop drinking. I would always laugh with
them and say something like I was using medicine
but not in the way they were thinking. If the person
then said that he wanted to stop alcohol use, I would
speak with the person and share my own experience,
strength, and hope from my recovery program. It was
over a period of two years that gradually we started
groups in different areas of the diocese and I accepted
invitations from parishes to come and talk with their
people about alcohol use and problems. Usually it
was a full two-day session and about seventy or eighty
persons would attend, some of whom I knew.*

And, of course, many of the attendees knew Jim
from his days of active alcoholism. The change in
him was obvious.

Jim had learned in recovery "not to invite myself into someone's life unless they asked me." He was ready to speak with anyone about alcoholism, but he did not impose himself on anyone. He was continuing to learn that the grace of receiving from others requires humility and acceptance. He was finding both in his new ministry. Jim's colleagues also noticed the change in him, again electing him to a position of leadership. This time around, there was no gap in the respect that others had for Jim and his own view of himself. That sense of peace was obvious to others and Jim began to lead in ways that he could not have previously imagined. He began to lead and give from his heart, ready and willing to receive through others the grace of God.

Four years into Jim's sobriety, the Conference of Tanzanian Bishops asked him to begin and direct a treatment center for Tanzanian priests. After praying over it, Jim agreed to begin the program after he completed some further studies. He returned to the United States on leave and received permission to attend the Summer School of Alcohol Studies, a three-week program held at Rutgers University in New Jersey.

Jim showed me a color photo of the group of people with whom he had studied at Rutgers. He looked wonderful in the photo, and he was in fact probably at the height of his physical health. The people in the picture had their arms around each others' shoulders like good friends who had been through something very meaningful together. These were people who knew the world of vulnerability as well as Jim did. He immediately felt at home with the group.

Jim read the course materials carefully, attended every lecture, never missed a Twelve Steps meeting. There was a drive in Jim to learn as much as possible, to make the best of this great opportunity, and to share what he had learned with others. He absorbed information everywhere. He was unafraid and unashamed. Jim followed through on lectures in the field of chemical dependency by sending letters that asked speakers for clarification of one of their points or recommendations about where and how to obtain more information on a topic. Jim wrote a letter to an expert on brain science asking for more details about the breakdown of brain tissue in alcoholism. The doctor responded with a detailed letter that Jim saved among his papers, referring to it from time to time to insure that he was reporting its information accurately.

The program at Rutgers was a turning point for Jim. For starters, "I realized I knew more than I was aware and became more confident to enter the field of chemical dependency ministry." The summer school also gave Jim a chance to catch up with himself, to match his experience with theory. He encouraged everyone interested in chemical dependence — including me — to attend the Rutgers program. I told Jim that given the age of my children, I could not go away for three weeks of school. Ever the second mate, Jim was not afraid of giving a direct order, and he gave me one about Rutgers. "Do it when your children get older." I suspect that my never having gone to Rutgers is neither the first nor the last direct order of Jim's that was disobeyed. He freely admitted that he had a terrible time with God not following Jim's will — or orders.

Conscious of the need for integration of knowledge he had obtained with his experience, Jim never lost sight of the fact that the most important thing he had to do was to take care of his own recovery. He felt renewed in his commitment to recovery and, with all appropriate anxiety, returned to Africa feeling up for the task of opening the first treatment center of its kind in Tanzania — if not in all of East Africa. He felt prepared to undertake a new ministry and was very enthusiastic to begin his work. It seemed as though his years in Tanzania and his recovery as an alcoholic were coalescing into a new and very meaningful expression. It was not until he actually began the work that Jim realized how much needed to be done in the area of alcoholism awareness and treatment.

As in so many countries, including the United States, there were social factors at work that encouraged heavy drinking. The general lack of understanding of alcoholism as a disease and the amount of work that clearly needed to be done gave Jim the sense that he was starting all over again in Tanzania. This time, however, it was not building, expanding the church, and covering hundreds of square miles on a motorcycle each week that confronted him. Jim's mission was to work for a shift in consciousness that would always depend on fidelity to his own recovery program. Working with alcoholism every day gave Jim no room to hide. He welcomed the openness and freely admitted that working with other chemically dependent people "kept me honest."

Jim found it more difficult than he expected to start the clergy program. He brought to the project the same singleness of purpose that had built churches and schools in the past. Like the nursing facility where Jim spent his last weeks, the treatment center was named for St. Teresa of Avila. Both mission sites draw courage and inspiration from their namesake, a woman who knew how to reform and change her outlook on life better than most. At St. Teresa's in Tanzania, Jim labored to set up a program for detoxification and residential treatment of afflicted clergy. The need for work on all levels of Tanzanian society became immediately apparent to Jim, as did the reality that he was never going to fully solve the problems.

Alcoholism is misunderstood and remains untreated all over the world, including in the United States. Jim's work was groundbreaking in a country where there was virtually no infrastructure in place for alcoholism education or treatment. Jim could not appeal to public service announcements or the printed word. His work needed to be one person at a time. As Jim wrote in the Maryknoll *Mission Forum* magazine in 1986:

> The chronic disease of alcoholism is pervasive in Tanzania, though it is very often not understood or recognized as a primary illness in itself. No government statistics are available on the problem; we have no detoxification centers and no treatment program exists under the Ministry of Health. In a valid sense, this particular healing ministry is in its pioneer days and therefore a great challenge.

Jim met on a grand scale the myths and misunderstandings that had so complicated his own recognition of alcoholism as a disease. He knew that providing information and a means of recovery would help restore the dignity of people afflicted by alcoholism. The philosophy of Alcoholics Anonymous is that two people who want to stop drinking and grow in their sobriety are all that are needed to begin an AA group. Soon Jim was working with education programs that helped farmers, teachers, medical people, anyone who was willing to come and listen. Anyone who was willing to talk about the impact of drinking in their lives found compassion and information at Jim's workshops. Jim spoke to major seminaries, religious sisters, parishes, and any group that invited him. He developed a two-day workshop that he gave in parishes, usually to groups of forty to seventy people who would travel from nearby villages to attend. Jim traveled to Kenya as a representative of Tanzania at a workshop on alcoholism. There he met other people who were becoming involved in the ministry of alcoholism in Africa. The meeting encouraged Jim to continue his work, often leaving the ninety-nine behind as he discovered the one person who most needed him. God seemed to put Jim in the right places at the right times to reach out with a prospect for healing the sickest alcoholic.

As the people gathered and listened to Jim, they began to understand the concept of alcoholism as a disease.

*Many could identify the symptoms of the disease in their own lives or in the lives of someone they loved. Once that happened, they easily began to talk with*

*the group about their own experience since they had
begun to understand that they are not bad people,
but rather very sick people and not sick because of
their own choice. By the end of the second day, those
who are interested in starting an AA or Al-Anon
group remain to hold their first meeting that very
afternoon.*

Jim learned to enlist the assistance and support of
parish priests and other authorities as these groups
formed. He knew that understanding and encour-
agement of the groups were extremely important in
the early stages of recovery. Jim also knew that the
groups would become self-reinforcing as the members began to feel better and experience serenity,
perhaps for the first time in their lives. AA was born
out of the insight that the only hope for alcoholics
seems to be in spiritual awakening where a higher
power — God, as defined by the individual — re-
stores the alcoholic to sanity. When the founders of
AA — Bill W. and his friend who was a physician,
alcoholics who had been given up on by friends, family, and medical professionals — began to work with
that premise, they both found recovery. Having experienced the spiritual awakening that led to peace
and having been privileged to witness it in others,
Jim saw the road to recovery as the incarnation of
the Paschal Mystery. He wrote:

*As someone who has studied the Bible for years, I have no question that the "Higher Power" of the Twelve Steps is the same God revealed in the life, death, and resurrection of Jesus Christ.*

Jim found in Tanzania that one by one and two by two a new life was being revealed. Jim shared in the powerlessness over alcohol, knew its devastation, and rejoiced in the rebirth. Through his work with alcoholics, Jim became one with Tanzanian people in their disease and their hope for recovery. Alcoholism crosses all borders and social classes, and the bond of recovery is more powerful than the disease. Working with other people who shared his disease helped Jim to understand his own ongoing conversion.

Years later Jim gave a retreat talk in Samoa, in which he reflected:

*The people whom God uses to teach a new spiritual way are often not recognized religious leaders but those who appear to be ordinary people. Men and women, carpenters like Jesus, tent makers like Paul, teachers of rhetoric like Augustine, soldiers like Ignatius Loyola, women like Mother Seton, or students of literature like Thomas Merton. Their methods have the smell of the earth and the sights and sounds of real life about them. The co-founders of AA were such people. They had been given up*

108

*on by everyone. Their disease had driven God out of their lives — like it drove God out of my life in a very real way. Admitting their own powerlessness, admitting the bankruptcy of their self-centeredness and the insanity of their self-destructive behavior, these spiritually crippled men and women turn to God and each other as their only hope. They develop a hunger for God. In becoming "weller than well" many of these men and women have found healing in their primary relationships, the peace of surrender, the humility and self-acceptance that follow confessions and making amends, and the joy and sense of purpose in doing God's will and sharing the hope and healing they are finding. God formed AA by taking a drunk stockbroker and a drunk doctor, both of whom seemed hopeless cases, and gathered around them a collection of apparently incurable alcoholics whose lives and relationships were in ruins. Out of this group God created a sensitive, caring, healing, spiritual community.*

Jim never ceased to marvel at the power of that community. Jim told me, "I believe in the AA slogan 'If you want to keep it, give it away.' You cannot grow in recovery by only focusing on yourself. It is in listening to others and reaching out to them that you keep the memories fresh and know that you are one drink away from disaster." If there was ever any doubt about the need for engagement in a human community, the knowledge of being that "one drink away" kept Jim focused. Having lived his sobriety for several years, Jim understood the retreat director's advice. He never believed that his recovery was completed or behind him. The choice for health was made over and over again, by the moment, the day, and the year. And he experienced just enough anxiety to keep him on his knees, humble enough to receive new gifts from God.

SEVEN

# *Waiting*

I HAVE LOST PEOPLE who died suddenly, and I have lost people who had long, lingering illnesses. As I watched the cancer eat away at Jim, I found myself cynically thinking of the advantages of sudden death and wondering how to put in an order for my own final process. I didn't want Jim to be going through what he was, and I was fairly certain that I could not face the process of death with his intentionality and courage. The thought scared me. Jim grew thinner each time that I saw him. I was desperate to do something for him. On some level I still wanted to believe that I could stop his death, or at least make it easier to witness.

Several times I asked Jim, "Can I bring you anything? Would you like a milkshake or ice cream?"

Pointing to the stash of food still on his nightstand Jim said, "No thanks. I have all the snacks I need. The nurses take good care of me. I'm going to get thin no matter what anybody does. I have everything I need. But come back and see me."

I told him that he could count on that. I was finding it remarkably difficult to accept that "just being"
with Jim was enough. He knew that he was dying; I
knew that he was dying. The surprise was that like so
many times in life, the actual experience was turning
out to be far longer, more powerful, and inescapably
transforming than the idea of it had been. Living that
truth was painful in that far more than I expected it
threw me face to face with my own fears and limitations. Jim keep telling me through his stories that
embracing such feelings and realities is the only path-
way to life. Sitting with Jim and his stories made
it clear to me that dying is at least as much work
as being born. Over and over in life we must pass
through a process as old and inexplicable as the tim-
ing of leaves changing colors. Every time that we do
so can seem like the first because what no one can
predict is the nature and demands of each rebirth.
We can only sit in its presence and realize that indeed our broken presence is all that we can provide.
When I accepted that with Jim, my energy was renewed so that I could be with him and learn more
about the perplexing realities of change. I also knew
in a different way that presence is at the heart of life's
meaning.

After working on alcoholism education and treatment for seven years in Tanzania, Jim accepted a

position back in the United States. His new assignment was to work with chemical dependence education within Maryknoll. Jim was aware as he prepared to leave Tanzania that it was unlikely he would return there to live. Yet he was at peace. The loose ends and feelings of shame that Jim carried back from Africa fourteen years earlier had been rewoven and healed. Jim had been very sick in Africa, and he had become "weller than well" there. He had completed an important part of the cycle of life. He had lived and witnessed the life, death, and resurrection of Jesus Christ.

Jim had gone to Africa originally with a keen sense of purpose and the knowledge that he was where God wanted him to be. Through the years he had faced failure, difficult odds, and the depths of his own illness. As he left Africa, he knew that he had barely made a dent in the field of chemical dependency treatment. Many of the circumstances in Tanzania were much worse than when Jim had arrived in 1955. When he left in 1987, AIDS was reaching epidemic proportions, grinding urban poverty was causing new alienation from land and family, and new types of drugs were being used by youth all over the country. Jim grieved for all of those changes and for the ministry that needed to be carried out. But he had done what was his to do. It was time to return to the place of his birth where, until an unexpected offer from Samoa came along, he expected to live out his remaining years.

"Whenever I came back to New York," Jim said, "I had to remember where I had stored my few boxes of things, catch up with my family, and learn to think like an American again. When I came back from Africa the last time, I felt more at home because I returned to my AA group." Jim was aging, and he knew it. He began to experience difficulties with his eyes that required drops, and his back rebelled against the strain and memory of all of those motorcycle rides across the African plain. At the same time, he felt more acutely the loss of both parents and four of his siblings. He particularly missed his sister Betty when he returned because until her death in 1973, he had always stayed at her house during his visits to New York. Within the next few years, he would lose three more of his siblings. There was little standing between Jim and his own mortality, which he chose to embrace long before his diagnosis with a terminal illness.

Jim noted each death and burial on the family history he kept. It was not until after his death that I looked at the family history and realized that he had written in "1998" as the year of his own death. He had no doubt made that notation while he was sick, yet its presence on the page symbolized that a bit of his own death was linked to each brother or sister who died before him. Jim was burying his own generation and that kept him cognizant of his own mortality. It also kept him very aware of the losses he had experienced over the course of his life, including the loss of Africa, which sometimes echoed within him. Jim wrote of his grief, again in a retreat talk that he gave in Samoa.

*In dealing with grief, what I am experiencing is sorrow, anguish, heartbreak, mourning, sadness, and suffering. None of these states is attractive or appealing. But I believe it is this path which can help me to identify more closely with the example of Christ's life and his attitude. Dealing with any loss, minor or major, in our lives can aid us in growing to understand our role of being human.*

To Jim, experiencing loss and grief are fundamental components of the human experience. Clearly he did not enjoy grief any more than anyone else, but he saw its value and experienced the process as leading to greater and deeper humanity. Touching more deeply into our humanity always meant for Jim that we were more deeply attuned to God. He had come to understand the vast difference between being weak and being vulnerable. The vulnerable, open heart always grieves in one way or another. Yet it is that heart upon which, as the prophet Jeremiah said, God writes his new law of love.

When reviewing his life, Jim no longer suffered grief in relationship to his alcoholism. He certainly recognized what the disease had cost him earlier in his life, but after years of recovery, Jim was much more in touch with the gifts that it had given him. When I asked Jim if he grieved for his cancer and his own death, he admitted that prior to his conversion in Las Vegas, his grief had been much more difficult to bear. As he became more in touch with the loving care of God, he came to a point where he said, "I don't like the process of getting there, but I think that dying will be fine." Then he pointed out that the process he didn't like was full of grief and letting go — just like life itself. While neither attractive nor appealing, that reality allowed Jim to call deeply upon his faith. "In the death of the seed," he reminded his retreatants, "comes new life."

Grief, however, is not always known to the mind. It renders its truths slowly, and in ways that can be both perplexing and quite clear. As Jim lost more conscious control to the cancer and the medication, a profound grief that he had acknowledged only around the edges began to be expressed from the depth of his soul. Over and over Jim asked, "Why did I try to do it alone?" I do not believe that he was referring to the cancer or to his decision to accept only palliative treatment. I think that he was breathing new life into what he had previously referred to as "Jim's plan" — the moving ahead quickly, not consulting, missing out on relationships, the loneliness. As he was dying, Jim was surrounded by people who loved him. His lament was perhaps the deepest surrender not only to "God's plan" but to an openness to express and heal the isolation that had cost him so much in life. When asking why he had tried to do it alone, Jim was in the presence of others. There were people there to hear his pain, and no one ran away. Rather, those who loved him stood still and witnessed his pain as in reality they had done all along.

Jim worked hard in his sobriety to bring that kind of presence and hope to others. He wrote articles, gave talks to anyone who would listen, and was called upon as a consultant in many interventions with chemically dependent individuals. The interventions helped bring alcoholics to recovery through the honest sharing of concern by individuals who loved them. Jim worked with families, friends, and concerned employers to help them understand that an intervention is about saving a life, not passing judgment. Interventions are often painful moments for everyone involved. For an alcoholic to move into recovery requires a major death to self, a willingness to accept that the situation is out of control. Since denial is at the heart of alcoholism, presenting that message in a caring way that an alcoholic is willing to accept requires patience, preparation, and prayer. Jim assisted people involved in interventions to work through their feelings so that what was presented to the alcoholic was less emotionally charged.

When discussing interventions with me, Jim always emphasized that no one other than a professional in the field needs to put themselves in the position of making a diagnosis of alcoholism. Recovery is not possible until individuals claim the alcoholism themselves. This is true whether one is involved in an individual interview or a planned intervention. For Jim, when the diagnosis of alcoholism finally came, it was such a relief that he immediately joined AA and began his recovery. That is not, however, always the case. Very often stronger intervention is needed, however unpleasant that initial event might be. The expression of concern and examples of how drinking has affected the lives of the people making the intervention are carefully worked out in advance. If the person is going to be taken in for evaluation and treatment, the appointment at the center has already been made when the group sits down together. Then all options and excuses are taken away from the alcoholic. "To save a life, you sometimes have to pull the rug out from under them," Jim said.

The rigor of working with people in moments of

intervention sometimes wore on Jim. Interventions are not natural settings for a man who grew up learning to avoid conflict. "I can always think of a more fun way to spend an afternoon," Jim admitted. He knew, however, that one of most painful parts of alcoholism is the isolation of it. Planning the intervention often broke the isolation of the family and friends of the alcoholic. Jim always referred those affected by the drinking of others to Al-Anon. There those wounded by the disease of another learned to reach out and recover in their own souls. Such recovery and interventions demonstrate a love that cannot be conned by the disease. Jim was quite aware that his presence at an intervention sometimes made it easier for alcoholics to admit their need for help. No one could look at Jim and deny that he spoke the truth about his own experience.

Jim had long since learned not to expect an immediate expression of gratitude for his participation in an intervention — at least not from the alcoholic. Many people later looked Jim up to thank him for his participation in the events that led them to recovery. Not all interventions are successful, and there were people who never forgave Jim and the others active in their intervention. Jim understood that as "the disease talking," and he prayed daily for those caught in the downward spiral of chemical dependency. He thanked God every day that people cared enough about him to bring his drinking to the attention of Maryknoll leadership. He thrived in the work and was well known in the local community as a resource person. Jim again discovered that God had a way of putting him where he needed to be of service. He witnessed the struggle of the people he reached out to and he rejoiced in their rebirth. It was during this period of his ministry that I had first met Jim and subsequently became his student. I was to learn through that experience that God also has a way of putting me where I needed to be so that I can find the piece of truth most pressing in my life at any given moment.

I had to that point been far less hopeful than Jim about the grief in my life, particularly the losses that were associated with my physical illness. I cycled through periods of time when I felt better, and I would scramble to make up for all of the time I had lost to the rheumatoid arthritis. Some part of me wanted to believe that a good day or better success with a new medication meant total remission. I would think to myself, "It is over, now let's get back to living." Invariably I crashed with great disappointment, grief, and anger. It was as if I had to accept the diagnosis over and over, and each time I tried to do so, there was a new round of grief about the limitations in my life. The pain itself evokes a grieving reaction in me because it makes me know that the disease is real and I am not in control of it. I admit to being a slow learner where my own life is concerned. I expect the stages of grief and acceptance to be linear, not cyclical. I feel like a failure every time I experience the same losses, or grieve for what I cannot do, be, or comprehend. The grief that seems to never end was caught in my body and its pain. In all honesty, I could not quite comprehend Jim's attitude about his own dying or his ongoing grief. When I sat silently with the reality, I thought his death was a mistake. Truth be told, I rather thought that all pain and death reflected something of a design error.

When I was an undergraduate, a professor teaching Elisabeth Kübler Ross's stages of dying posed the question, "How do you think that you would work through the stages if you were told right now that you had six months to live?" I was twenty years old. I admitted I knew that if I was terminally ill at that age, I would never reach the point of peace and resolution before my death. Furthermore, I expected to go through all eternity insulted by the idea of my death and angry at having been cheated out of a long and productive life. My professor suggested that maturity might change my point of view. I remember thinking that the only thing that would change my point of view was another seventy unencumbered years on the planet, and even then I knew that maturing by that time was not a sure thing.

Living has taught me that nothing is guaranteed in life, especially how many years one will live or in what condition. Maturity did help me to understand that the laws of the universe were not written by me, and life can be brutally unfair. But it was Jim Lenihan who actually accomplished the formidable task of teaching me that the fear of being human is at the root of most internal rebellion. What is more human than to suffer limitation, to get sick, to die and rise. My silent assumption, however, was that the usual rules of life did not apply to me. Priding myself — and therein lies the key — on strength and resiliency, it has been hard for me to recognize the opportunity contained within my experience of physical and mental illness. Remembering who we are as human beings, taking care of ourselves and each other, suffering and rising, why should it be otherwise? Jim's dying reminded me often that there is no reason any of us should feel that we are exempt from the trials of human life. My problem with grief was that I fought it rather than letting it lead me to a new understanding that being human was enough for God, and it is surely enough for me.

Sometimes familiar losses demand fresh tears as we cycle through them and know them as part of our living flesh. Initially that new way of knowing can feel like a failure of a long-sought resolution. More accurately, the new tears are an opportunity to heal on a deeper level and to understand loss as it relates to a different stage of life. Jim frequently quoted the statement of St. Irenaeus, "The glory of God is a person fully alive." To him that statement was testimony to the power of God working through the human person. If we fail to embrace our humanity, with all of its pain, uncertainty, and lack of guarantees, we cannot be fully alive and thus cannot experience the joy of God's presence within and through us. Jim believed that Irenaeus called us to greater humility in the true sense of the word. A key element of that type of humility is to assume only that God will be present, regardless of the circumstances of life. With those ideas in mind, I began to let go of my claim to a long, productive, unencumbered life. Remarkably, the joy of what is real and lasting becomes much more apparent to me when those fantasies and expectations are put in their proper place. When I stopped stamping my foot in regard to things I could not control, I was amazed at how much energy became available to me. Being so stubborn about the frailties of life can wear a person down to nothing.

# EIGHT

# *Angels Unaware*

WHEN I WALKED into his room at St. Teresa's, Jim was reaching for the phone. "I was just going to call you," he said, "and suddenly the angel appeared."

I answered, "Well, now we know how long it takes for thought to travel. But if you are looking for an angel, you might want to make another call."

Jim laughed. "No, you are the angel."

"Of death?" I ventured.

"Oh, no. The angel of life. But I do need to tell you that people around here are starting to get nervous if they see you coming toward them. They think that you might know something that the doctor didn't tell them. Being seen with me gives you a bad reputation."

"Remind me to start carrying a white candle as I walk down the hall." We both laughed.

"Once people know that you are dying," Jim said, "the relationship changes. Some people are coming by to tell me things that they want me to know before I die. Others stop in, shoot me a wave from the door-

125

way, and get out as soon as possible. I don't know what bothers them more, that I am dying or that I have cancer and that makes it really obvious. Boy, people are afraid of disease and death."

"No kidding." I said, well aware of my own hesitations. "Are you afraid?"

"Oh, I'm starting to wonder about what happens in the end, whether or not my visions of heaven are true. Mostly I think of it as passing over into a new stage in life. I think death is going to be a beautiful thing, surrender to God. I've had some practice at that after all. I'm expecting to see some people in heaven that I have been missing for a long time. I am facing in a new way what I have taught my whole life as a priest about life coming from death. It's different when you're the one who is dying. I told God in Las Vegas that he would have to help me because I've never been physically dying before. A new experience."

"I think God is teaching you just fine."

Jim, demonstrating his somewhat legendary inability to take a compliment answered, "Yeah, but you're on drugs."

"Steroids make me cranky, not blind," I said with feigned defensiveness.

"Well, thank God we cleared that up," Jim said.

"What were you calling me about?" I asked, suddenly feeling how very much I would miss this man.

"I want to make sure that you understand about gratitude."

Somehow that should not have surprised me, but it did.

"Okay," I answered, "tell me about gratitude." And I thought to myself about how much he already had.

Jim asked me to reread something that he had written:

*I have come to realize more deeply how other people, family, relatives, friends, and the people I served, affected my own life. In my early years I became shy, open to concern about others and not taking care of nurturing myself. This pattern continued as I was an adult. It was only when I fell flat on my face with my alcoholism that I began to acquire a new awareness in my life regarding myself, God, and others. I can clearly see the changes that have taken place in my life as a result of being fully involved in my recovery program, which is the first priority in my life. It is the treasure that has given me this awareness to understand myself better and thus to understand fellow human beings. It has helped me today to be aware of the proper domains in my life. I have a responsibility in our human domain. I do not have the responsibilities of God, and I must ful-*

fill my role as a human being and a child of God.
I realize that being human entails "growing pains"
that get my attention and help me refocus on what
is really important in the one day I have been given
at a time.

Like many other people I could come up with a
long list of things I am grateful for, but I always
want to work from that list to show God and others
my gratitude by my behavior. I am grateful to have
been born into the family of the Lenihans. Grateful that during the latter '20s and '30s we were not
as affected by the great depression as others were. I
am grateful I was born in this country. I am glad I
had my war experiences and training at Kings Point
Academy. Grateful for my priesthood and Maryknoll. Grateful for the thousands and thousands of
people who have come into my life both in this country and overseas. I am glad that I am Jim and not
someone else. God needs each of us, and to reject
myself would be an insult to God. I am grateful that I
have had a good and interesting life with many blessings and much forgiveness received from God and
others. Above all, I am grateful for my alcoholism
and all that it has taught me.

I asked Jim to say more about his gratitude for
alcoholism. He said unexpectedly, "You know what
that is about. Aren't you grateful for your disease?

Hasn't it taught you things that you would not have learned any other way?" It happened that he asked that question on a day when, in fact, I was not particularly grateful for the disease. And I really did not immediately see why I should be. That day I just hurt. There are days when the pain is all that there is and that must become its own way of being. I recognized, however, what Jim was saying. Gratitude for the disease itself requires looking beyond the immediate experience and claiming what gifts lie in the seemingly unproductive dust.

After thinking for a moment, I said to Jim, "I believe that being ill has made me more compassionate. I'm less quick to judge others because I know that I don't know the truths of their lives. And I think that being ill has made me believe more in God — not as an abstraction but in the constancy of day-to-day struggle and life." Jim nodded his head while I continued. "There were so many things that I thought were so important — ambitions, ideas, control, pride. The disease lays me low and I know something more about who I am in the world, who I am in relationship to God. I know about limitation and disappointment. I know a bit more about how concrete hope can be. Mostly I know that I must be in caring relationships with other people — that not much else matters." Those indeed are gifts I know and claim in myself and could certainly recognize in

Jim. I was glad that he asked the question because it broadened my immediate perspective.

I could not articulate at that time something that Jim was then in the middle of teaching me. When we become ill, suffer a great loss, or are for any other reason not fully in control of life, we inhabit a world that often feels invisible except to others who live there. Strength and self-reliance have been misconstrued as the normal and admirable way of being in the world. This is particularly true in the small part of the world where affluence can cushion the reality and appearance of human suffering. Once we have experienced the phone call in the middle of the night that changes everything, the positive blood test or biopsy, the loss of a loved one, addiction or any of the difficulties of human life, we become vulnerable in ways that are hard to reconcile with previous expectations. Something has not worked right, be it our own immune systems or our notion of a powerful, protective God. We cross over into a different experience and understanding of life where vulnerability is immediate and pervasive. A new sight becomes available. Priorities shift and rearrange. Nothing is assumed about the guarantee of a future. Gratitude is not likely to be the first feeling experienced during the shift.

When in the midst of discovering that vulnerability, the world that believes in its own strength can become very annoying. I can recall overhearing conversations at the health club after my diagnosis and being furious at the concentration on physical beauty and the assumption of health. Sometimes I wanted to scream in the locker room, "Do you think that your health is guaranteed? Do you think that you will always be strong?" I knew the questions to ask because they were born of assumptions that previously underwrote my own life. One of the most powerful losses I have experienced with a chronic illness is the failure of confidence and control — the vivid knowledge that I have a disease that does not bend to my will. I must, in fact, bend to its demands.

The secret most of us are keeping is that we all have at least one foot in the vulnerable world most of the time. It is where we really live, love, and experience our humanity. While the frayed boundaries of this human experience may be tucked under or hidden, God's mercy and presence are abundant there. When denial of our humanity has failed, God calls us into the deeper experience of compassionate relationship with each other. The world of vulnerability is the domain of the human heart and soul. Until we have traveled there through circumstances beyond our control, most of us would rather impersonate strength. Yet it is in the broken heart, the humanity that is changed by loss and limitation, that true conversion takes place. It is a powerful thing to gather around brokenness; AA was for Jim and many others that kind of community. Sitting with Jim as he was dying allowed me to experience my own vulnerability more fully, not simply as a source of pain, but as the grace of an unseen earth where, to one degree or another, all human beings really live. Claiming myself as part of that vulnerable planet turned out to be a huge relief. Only then could I begin to understand that God's love is not distributed on the basis of accomplishments or the strength of one's armor. Ever present, the love is known when the will to rule is shattered and humanity is curiously revealed in full. As Jim said in reference to his alcoholism, that experience is "one of the great gifts of my life."

The word was definitely out that Jim was dying. He had many visitors, received a great deal of mail, and answered numerous phone calls. Jim's nieces and nephews came to visit him and he was in frequent telephone contact with his sister Theresa and his brother Bernard. His AA sponsor and members of his group brought the program to him when Jim was too sick to make a trip to a meeting. Jim was contacted by many people who wanted to thank him for the role he had played in their lives. Jim was surprised by many of these letters and visits. He had been influential for so many people — through example, small acts of kindness, and direct intervention — that he had forgotten the details. As people made contact with him, he rediscovered relationships and meaning as if he were stumbling across his father's photographs and recognizing for the first time the faces and meanings captured there. Jim was coming to know how much he had done in the lives of other people, how much gratitude people felt toward him, and how much he was loved. He was surprised every time.

That Jim was so gracious in receiving his visitors, phone calls, and letters was a great gift. The story that I wanted to get on paper had already been written in the lives of other people. Jim was extraordinarily generous and hospitable in receiving what other people needed to tell him. He let people talk at their own pace and he listened very well. Sometimes he received so many visitors that he was exhausted. He would turn no one away because he was aware of how important it was for other people to tell him what they needed to say. A hospice volunteer helped him to answer the letters, to send his last words of love to people he cared about deeply. One of the letters he wrote was to an internal Maryknoll publication; it described a visit of great importance to Jim. When he showed me the typed copy to read, he said that he knew this was the last piece of writing that he would ever do. It was published two weeks before his death; Jim was correct that he would not have the strength to write another word.

*As I reside here at St. Teresa's for care in dealing with my terminal cancer, I find many blessings that I see coming through visits to me by fellow Maryknollers and people who have had long association with Maryknoll. On a Sunday afternoon about two weeks ago, a young man named John came to visit with me. We had not seen nor been in contact for over twenty-one years. When we met, he was one of about thirteen young men who were involved in Maryknoll's vocation discernment program. The late Father Joe Rickert and I were doing development and vocation work. That was how John and I met.*

*As he sat down with me that Sunday, he told me he had just come from an informal gathering at the Maryknoll Center of people who had participated in the 1977 discernment process. One of the men in that group who was ordained for Maryknoll arranged the meeting. He told John that I was now residing here at St. Teresa's for medical care. John then told me how grateful he was to me for help that I gave him during that year of discernment. John had the same experience as the man from Geresene. Jesus led him to a different life than what he originally had in mind. John told me that he has never forgotten those times and occasions we met, either one on one,*

*with his family, or as part of the discernment group.
John told me that twelve of the thirteen people who
were invited that Sunday had attended. Two things
impressed me in his visit. He came to thank me and
he had kept that gratitude in his life all those many
years. Secondly, that gratitude had developed during
his own life so that one can see today an attitude and
a gratefulness that affects his present life. For myself,
listening to John that Sunday afternoon in my room
here at St. Teresa's gave me a feeling and awareness
of how we affect those around us as we try to do
whatever we think is our work. John has a peace in
his heart and will through his acceptance that there
are many gifts in ministry. Those graces he received
twenty-one years ago have continued to grow and
will be a gift to the world.*

Jim was really surprised that John had taken the
time to find him and thank him for his influence and
assistance. Jim never expected to see John again, nor
did he fully realize the important role that he had
played in John's life. It was time to remind Jim of
his teaching on humility. "You've played an important role in many people's lives," I told him. "Now
is the time to accept their love and gratitude." Jim
smiled. He was getting tired, and I told him that I
didn't want to wear him out. Jim asked me to stay
a few more minutes because he said that my visits

gave him energy. It was my turn to be humble. We sat in silence for some time during which both of us gave and received. It was a deeply sacred moment in which I experienced healing of my need to do something or to fight off the grief I felt. After we had sat there for some time, I asked Jim to give me his blessing. He did, and the only word I could say — like so many other people — was thanks.

# NINE

# Summer's End

AUGUST WAS SHIFTING the light, reminding the northern half of the world that, like all seasons, summers are temporary. Even with that knowledge, most of us feel a touch of grief as the days grow measurably shorter and the challenges of autumn become more immediate. For Jim, the brevity of the summer reminded him of the passing of precious hours and days. Jim's strength was working against him in many ways. His body was giving up slowly; a heart strengthened by years of walking in ten-mile clips was beating strongly even as the cancer ravaged him. Jim was still hoping to be able to attend the eighteenth anniversary of his sobriety on August 30. My family was going to the Jersey shore the same week.

I told Jim that I would be going on vacation at the end of the month, and I wanted to go over some of the outlines before I left. He was still sitting in his armchair, his nightstand behind him and the need to move into a wheelchair more pressing with each day. "That's fine with me," he said. "And I expect to be here when you come back unless something unexpected happens. The doctor thinks that I will live for several more weeks — maybe even a couple of months."

"Do you believe him?" I asked.

"I'm not quite sure what to think. I'm probably not the most objective judge."

"There are two things that medical science can't tell you with any certainty," I said to him. "They're guessing what day the baby will be born and they are really guessing about how long you have before you die."

Jim smiled. "Well, that fits. I guess it really doesn't make any difference because all that I can do is live it one day at a time anyway. False humility aside, I've gotten pretty good at that over the years."

"I suppose that you have," I answered. Living one day, one moment at a time is a crucial component of AA.

Jim had written in one of his outlines:

*Spiritual growth happens only in the present moment as we surrender ourselves, as we are, to the presence of God. If we are obsessed with either the past or future, it is likely that we are trying to play God. Spiritual growth is an ongoing process. Daily prayer and meditation and attention to our own spiritual needs are ways we exercise our spiritual muscles and grow stronger in our daily lives. This is the moment God has given us. It is easy to let up on trying to grow spiritually. Our growth in spirituality will be shown in maintaining the proper balance between the outer world where we work, worry, and rush about and our inner world where we reflect, accept, and trust.*

Jim's muscles were strong from years of spiritual practice. He had grown in acceptance and trust to a point that he inspired those qualities in others. He reminded me as we talked that slowing down and recognizing that we don't have to do everything on our own releases the tension and isolation that leads to closing off our hearts and reaching for the substance of choice.

Jim and I discussed the assignments in his priesthood after he worked as a chemical dependency counselor. He became the first Vicar for Retirement in Maryknoll, as position which gave him particular responsibilities for older priests and brothers. Jim himself was sixty-eight and had been mining the treasures of his own aging process. He pointed out to me a retreat talk that he had given about aging.

*When we approach the later stages of our life journey, many of us might focus only on the possible losses we may experience: loss of vision, hearing, memory, health, and friends. It is necessary then that we be able to call on the resources of faith to help us live through our losses.... Our hope comes from dealing with loss in our lives which is done by trusting God. We also, each time we are in the process of dealing with loss in our lives, must remember that we are not alone in our journey of life. In dealing with each loss we gain experience and grow in trusting God. In the Book of Isaiah it is written: "In your old age I shall still be the same, when your hair is gray I shall still support you. I have already done so, I have carried you, I shall still support and deliver you" (Isaiah 46:4).*

Having helped others to recognize that aging is part of the cycle of life, Jim decided after three years in the position that it was time to retire himself. Before he could fully adjust to retirement, he received an invitation from his seminary classmate, Bishop Quinn Weitzel, the first bishop of the Samoa–Pago Pago Territory of American Samoa. Jim was surprised by the invitation, and by then far more experienced in the art of discernment than he had been in 1947, he agreed to be a resident priest. He arrived in January of 1996 planning to stay three years. His part-time apostolate was something totally new for him. He became the chaplain of a girls high school, conducted a number of retreats which have been quoted here, and worked with diocesan priests and students. As always, he was available to anyone who needed assistance with a chemical dependency problem.

The three-year assignment became two years when the diagnostic x-ray was taken. "And you know the rest of the story," Jim told me. I nodded.

Jim said that he had met with a seminary classmate to plan his funeral liturgy. Two of Jim's nephews are funeral directors. On their last visit to Jim, they had offered to prepare his body for burial. Jim did not want to create a problem by varying from Maryknoll's usual funeral director, but he was deeply touched by his nephews' offer. Jim had lived in countries where preparing the body for burial is the final care given by the family. It is done in a spirit of love. By allowing his nephews to care for his body, Jim was living out that spirit. It was also special to Jim because his nieces and nephews were so important to him. Throughout their lives he had followed their growth, the details of their lives, and embraced their children. Jim had been visited frequently at St. Teresa's by his nieces and nephews and their children. Those visits gave him the joy that comes from knowing that the world and family will be born anew and go on without us.

Discussing his funeral arrangements, Jim quipped, "Now that I have veterans benefits, maybe I should take them up on their burial plot. I could have used help with my education instead." But had that help been given, Jim might never have spent the summer at sea that was the turning point in his life and vocation. Besides, Jim said, "Maryknoll is my home, I want to be buried here."

He told me to go on vacation, have a great time, and to come back to see him when I returned. Talking about his funeral arrangements was the last long conversation Jim and I would ever have.

While I was gone, Jim and several of his friends from Africa held an anointing service in his room at St. Teresa's. Jim chose the prayers and the scripture reading and invited everyone to join in the anointing. He was lucid enough to be a full participant in the service.

"When people talk about the courage and heroism in Jim's death," said Father Tom McDonnell, "they tend to emphasize his decision to forgo treatment and the bravery in the face of his pain. Jim's real gift to us was that he allowed the process of his dying to become a channel of grace for all the people around him. The anointing service was a powerful, sacred moment when he invited us all to share in his death and promise of resurrection. It was a stunning experience. I doubt if it was the last time that Jim was anointed, but at that service he brought a consciousness and openness that is a rare gift. I will never forget it."

When I returned, Jim was in a much weakened state. He had declined rapidly in a short time, partially because the medication had been changed to try to address his excruciating pain. The Phelps Hospital hospice team worked with Jim and the St. Teresa's staff to try to make him as comfortable as possible. The doctor increased the medication, which first made Jim nauseous and then drowsy. A fitful sleep followed. Jim could still speak, but very softly and in short sentences. He had missed his anniversary AA meeting because he was too sick to go. Part of the meeting had come to him by way of his sponsor and a member of his home group visiting to acknowledge and celebrate with him eighteen years of sobriety. When I visited Jim, he said to me with some effort, "How are you feeling?"

"Fine," I answered.

"Me, too."

Seeing him in so much pain ask about me first and still want to make a joke made me unbelievably sad.

Jim's sister Theresa and her husband, Ed, came from Florida to join the Maryknollers who sat vigil with Jim. Theresa and Ed participated in the prayer and liturgical life of St. Teresa's during their sojourn. They already knew many of the priests and brothers living there. Jim instructed Theresa on a few last things, including calling me to come over and pick up a computer disk that he thought I should have. The disk contained outlines of the retreat talks from Samoa. The predominant theme of those talks was surrender.

The visit in which I picked up the disk was the last time I saw Jim alive. He slipped away a few days later, his death as much a blessing as his life. Everything he had believed, lived, and taught emphasized that this time the homecoming would not be bittersweet. I was grateful that his suffering had ended, and at the same time I already missed him. Death, even when a blessing, creates a chasm between the known and the unknown, the embrace and the trepidation. I really did not want to let Jim go. Mercifully, he did not go beyond the reach of the living heart.

Jim's funeral was just as he had planned it — a great celebration of life. The leadership of Maryknoll honored his request that at the time of his death his recovery from alcoholism be publicly known as a means of offering hope to others. A section of his letter to the leadership was included in the biography letter sent around the Maryknoll world. His nephews took loving care of Jim's body. The Lenihans gathered at the wake and funeral as did Maryknoll priests, brothers, sisters, and lay missioners. Jim was remembered that day in Tanzania, Samoa, and beyond. It was a beautiful fall day in New York.

The leaves began to reach their peak the following week. There was an empty space in my heart that I recognized as a grief that would need to follow its own trajectory. I missed him. I missed our conversations. I missed going to visit him. I didn't know how I was ever going to do justice to what he wanted to say. I prayed to him. The leaves reminded me of Jim's transformation. My summer with him was over, but the emergence of life from death had happened anew. I walked a lot in the late afternoon — ostensibly to keep my joints healthy but also to have time for remembering. Though I continued to believe that the moment of Jim's death was a great blessing for him, for anyone who knew him, the ache promised to remain for some time.

Around the feast of All Saints/All Souls, I had a dream in which I saw Jim looking very healthy and alive. He was standing by a banquet table piling food high on his plate. I was surprised to see him. I said to him, "You are dead. I saw you get so thin, and I went to your funeral."

He looked at me with bright eyes and said, "Oh, hell. You didn't think that was the end of the story did you? Have a little faith, for crying out loud."

Whatever the source of my dream, it helped me to

realize that I had to allow faith to enter my heart at the same level as the grief. Jim was in the fullness of life. I had to get out of the way and believe in that transformation for Jim, for myself, and for anyone who stands in the vulnerable world and needs to know that there is more to the story than pain.

Jim's decision not to undergo treatment for his cancer was an appropriate one given his age and physical condition. He was the first to say, however, that for other people facing cancer under different circumstances "fighting like hell" would be the right thing to do. Wisdom lies in knowing the difference between what must be accepted and what must be fought against with all of one's strength. Having achieved that level of wisdom was one of Jim's major human accomplishments. Though the cancer ravaged him and took the life of his body, Jim left this world a whole human being. He had been deeply healed through his recovery. There is a tendency to think of healing as erasure of illness, pain, or brokenness. That is a false notion. Healing is wholeness that comes through embracing one's humanity — its limitations and its gifts — and as a result joining the human race. I have seen people who were cured and not healed; they carried bitterness about the insult of their illness and struggle for years. At the same time, healing sometimes comes to the physically and mentally ill though their disease might remain the same. Healing is an ongoing process because life is an ongoing process. It comes to the soul, connects us to each other, and never ends in this life. Healing is nourished by faith in an unseen "rest of the story." It cannot grow in the proud of heart and very often, the deepest form of healing in no way resembles a physical cure. We begin to heal when we know that God is here, even in the midst of realities and events that we will never be able to fully understand.

Another summer is ending. I am looking out at the Atlantic Ocean on Labor Day, taking a deep breath before stepping into the demands of September. I am feeling better after a change in medication for the arthritis; my spirit is strong, the depression under control. I am grateful. I feel blessed by understandings that have been renewed in the hours spent poring over Jim's handwriting. It has been a gift to remember him in such detail. I fight my illness less now, embrace vulnerability a bit more. Julius Nyerere was right about the nature of individual and collective independence: it is most viable when based on interdependence. Paradoxically, accepting the reality of illness has made available to me a new experience of health and happiness. The gift of happiness has been given to me by many people, including Jim. He taught me that all of us must live with something.

Transformation begins when we also live through whatever the "it" may be, not by way of endurance but as an experience of grace. Living through is not just survival, it is allowing the truths we might most seek to hide to become the source of illumination. It was that spirit that allowed Jim to call alcoholism "the greatest gift of my life." Remembering his story, talking about Jim with others, and feeling his spirit close at hand has led me to know that the gift he received was the one he gave away. What could have been the source of shame and isolation became the conduit for grace and redemption. Such was the miracle, the blessing, and the stunning achievement of Jim's life. His gift will always be near at hand, in days of shifting light and gratitude so sacred and elemental that it is cause for awe. And for that, I will forever be grateful.

# Acknowledgments

I AM INDEBTED to my husband, Richard, and my children, Michael and Patrick, who encourage my passion and endure my distraction when I am writing. Their support and patience means the world to me. I am grateful for the assistance given by Pat and John Hoffman, Wayne Fitzpatrick, Gary Hellman, my colleagues past and present at Maryknoll, Michael Leach, Orbis Books, Maryknoll Social Communications, and the Saturday morning prayer group. I offer thanks to Theresa Lenihan Lieber for her gracious spirit and kindness to me. Finally, I thank the generations of people whose vision, generosity, and support have given life to Maryknoll — the Society, the Congregation, and the Association of the Faithful. Without them, there would be no story to tell.

*Of Related Interest*

## Lives of Service
*Stories from Maryknoll*
Text and photographs by Jim Daniels
128 pages, color photos, 10 ½ x 11
ISBN 1-57075-308-3, hardcover

This beautifully illustrated book takes readers
on an inspiring journey of faith and discovery
inside the mission of Maryknoll.

## Dialogue of Life
*A Christian among Allah's Poor*
by Bob McCahill
128 pages, photographs, 5 ⅜ x 8 ¼
ISBN 1-57075-066-1, paperback

The inspiring testament of a priest and missioner
who for twenty years has pursued an unusual
witness among the poor of Bangladesh.

## The Misfit
*Haunting the Human — Unveiling the Divine*
by Larry Lewis
196 pages, 5 ⅜ x 8 ¼
ISBN 1-57075-122-6, paperback

A moving story of how God breaks through the
aridity of human hearts.

*Also by*

# Teresa Rhodes McGee

### *Ordinary Mysteries*
*Rediscovering the Rosary*
128 pages, photos, 5 ⅜ x 8 ¼
ISBN 1-57075-363-6, paperback

Recovers the rosary for a new generation.
Both practical and inspirational, *Ordinary Mysteries*
offers contemporary meditations on the
fifteen mysteries of the rosary.

Please support your local bookstore,
or call 1-800-258-5838

For a free catalog, please write us at
## Orbis Books, Box 308
## Maryknoll, NY 10545-0308
or visit our website at www.orbisbooks.com

Thank you for reading *Jim's Last Summer.*
We hope you enjoyed it.